Adrian Lan

INFAMOUS
CON ARTISTS
AND SCAMMERS

*History's Craziest
True Crime Stories*

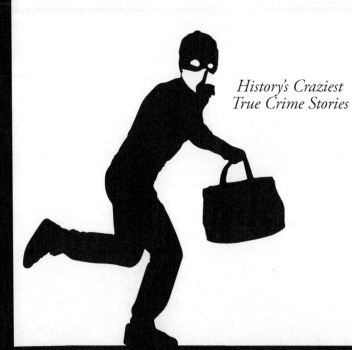

Imprint
Authors: Adrian Langenscheid, Benjamin Rickert, Caja Berg

ISBN: 978-3-98661-101-9

1st edition March 2023
© 2023 True Crime International/ Stefan Waidelich,
Zeisigweg 6, 72212 Altensteig, Germany

Cover image: © Freepik-Freepik.com Premium License 7 Feb. 2023
Cover design: by Marynart @Fiverr.com

CONTENTS

Preface *1*

Chapter 1: A villa with chimpanzees 5

Chapter 2: Miss Unknown 17

Chapter 3: High above 33

Chapter 4: The strength of a woman 45

Chapter 5: One million sorrows 63

Chapter 6: The House of Cards...95

Chapter 7: Prince Dubai 115

Chapter 8: Girl, you know it's true....................................129

Chapter 9: News from the beyond 143

Chapter 10: The Prince of Poyais......................................167

Chapter 11: The Romanian box 183

Chapter 12: Fine feathers make fine birds..........................197

Concluding words of the author..*213*

Newsletter: *214*

Recommendations...*215*

True Crime International: *216*

I CAN CALCULATE THE MOVEMENT
OF CELESTIAL BODIES, BUT NOT THE
OCCASIONAL ABNORMAL BEHAVIOR OF
PEOPLE.

- *Isaac Newton (1642 - 1727)*
Astronomer, mathematician, and physicist -

PREFACE

Brazen impostors, unscrupulous fortune tellers, and cunning tricksters; the craziest, most bizarre, and unbelievable criminal cases in history are waiting for you on the coming pages. It shamelessly puts its finger in the wound of human naivety.

Stunned, baffled, and shaking your head, you will marvel in disbelief at the madness to which the creativity and clever audacity of manipulative narcissists can seduce people.

Experience the fascinating story of a fake tsar's daughter, or learn more about the man who invented an entire country in order to finance his life of wealth and luxury by selling it. Read about a fake Saudi prince and about one of the richest women in the world, who stands up to her brazen blackmailer. Dark machinations surrounding fake pop stars and famous television shows are also exposed in a ruthless manner.

In the twelve chapters that follow, you can expect a riveting collection of true stories of intrigue, lies, and betrayal that will shock, leave you speechless, and amuse you in equal measure. This amazing journey through history will take you to some of the greatest con artists and deceivers of all time and will challenge your imagination. Be prepared for an extraordinary reading experience!

MANY ROADS LEAD TO WEALTH, YET MOST OF THEM ARE DIRTY.

- Peter Rosegger (1843–1918),
  Austrian writer and poet -

CHAPTER 1

A VILLA WITH CHIMPANZEES

Like lukewarm coffee, the sea breeze blows through the narrow streets of the Italian village of Grimaldi, carrying with it the scent of salt water on its way. The village stretches across the foot of a mountain lined with green vegetation, lying directly on the coast of the Ligurian Sea. Here and there, the wind passes excitedly, chattering children pointing their index fingers at the store windows. Vendors present ashtrays in the shape of a chimpanzee. In his right hand, he holds a pistol, emblazoned below the phrase: 'Come here, Voronoff, if you dare!

"Mommy, when are we going to see the monkeys?" a girl asks, gazing up at her mother expectantly in the face of the blazing sun.

"Soon, darling. But only if you behave well," the woman replies.

The girl does not know nor understand what dark cause lies behind her wish and the sale of the souvenirs. She is simply looking forward to marveling at the animals up close.

A few kilometers away, a man with a bushy moustache, high forehead, and big nose is just entering the monkey cage on his estate. He is wearing a white coat underneath a black suit with a white shirt and dark tie. Under the curious gaze of onlookers beyond the walls, he picks out one of the chimpanzees and brings it outside. The animal shrieks and squirms in desperation, but the man's grip has tightened around the small body like a vice. Slowly, the man strolls toward his villa, where the monkey faces a grisly fate.

54 years earlier, in July 1866, a boy named Serge Voronoff was born in a small Russian village. The family of several children lives in poor circumstances, despite their father Abram's occupation as a distiller. Serge, however, stands out from the simple family picture. He is considered highly gifted at an early age and, after graduating from school at 18, goes to Paris to study medicine.

At the time of the "Belle Epoque," the city of love already had a population of around three million and was experiencing a cultural upswing. This was due to the construction of the Eiffel Tower, Impressionism, Art Nouveau, and important personalities such as the composer Claude Debussy.

However, the beauty and diversity of Paris also have their price. You only really belong if you can afford the expensive life along the Seine. And that is precisely Serge's plan; he, too, wants to be a part of this romantic world. To achieve this, Paris University offers him a number of opportunities. The most respected researchers of his time practiced there, such as Charles-Édouard Brown-Séquard, who was the first person ever to map the human spinal cord. Although the 72-year-old neurologist is highly regarded in the medical world, he harbors a bizarre secret: to counteract the aging process, he injects himself with a mixture of testicular and sperm extracts from guinea pigs and street dogs. He knows that the genitals of male creatures must contain something that can slow down the natural aging process. Brown-Séquard's early form of hormone treatment doesn't make him any younger, but it lays the foundation for the career of one of his protégés.

Bald surgeon Alexis Carrel, who later even wins a Nobel Prize for his work on vascular suturing and vascular and organ transplants, is also an important guiding figure for Serge. For Serge to gain practical experience in medicine, Carrel advises him to go to Egypt, which the now 30-year-old immediately follows.

Under the oppressive heat in the land of the pharaohs, he becomes a personal physician at the court of the Khedives and, during this work, makes a discovery that will later make him famous. On the estate of the king live so-called "eunuchs," men who were subjected to castration in their childhood. When Serge takes a closer look at their anatomy, he finds that emasculation seems to affect the skeleton, musculature, nervous system, and psychological development. In addition, it leads to the absence of puberty and, consequently, intimate hair growth, voice change, and an expression of the genitals. So if the removal of the testicles has an effect on the human body, could it also be that it reacts to the addition of those accordingly?

For 14 years, Serge remained in Egypt and worked as a doctor, but his theory about testicular transplantation simply wouldn't let him go. However, since his strictly scheduled workday did not allow him any private research, he returned to France in 1912. There he immediately began his experiments but initially limited himself to animal experiments. Following the example of Carrel's transplants, he wanted to discover what the addition of testicles would do to them. And, who knows: perhaps this method could also be transferred to humans.

Serge's approach may seem strange, but it was by no means unusual at the time. In general, the turn of the century is marked by medical progress; within a very short time, vaccines against rabies as well as dystonia - a neurological movement disorder - and cholera are developed, the infant mortality rate is halved within a generation, and mankind's faith in medicine continues to grow. Because of these rapid successes, scientists begin experimenting with bizarre things - perhaps a miracle cure for disease will also develop. Therefore, the motto of the research of that time was to leave no stone unturned.

However, the doctors practice all these experiments exclusively in their spare time. They all have the incentive to advance medical knowledge and find new ways to cure a wide variety of diseases while pursuing their normal existence as doctors during the day. Serge, for example, successfully transplants skin from a cadaver to a burn victim and transplants the thyroid gland of a monkey to a short-statured man with hypothyroidism. Incredible as it sounds, the procedure is having its desired effect. The thyroid gland works, and the young man grows to normal size. So Serge and his colleagues are not crazy professors who find fun in dabbling in outlandishness; there is always - according to the times - a serious, medical thought behind their experiments.

But why is Voronoff so obsessed with his idea of testicular transplantation? Is he really just interested in advancing medical science? Or is there something else behind it? Some believe it has something to do with the 44-year-old's wife at the time. They say the couple could not have children due to Serge's inability to conceive. Therefore, it would stand to reason that he would develop the testicular transplant - if it works - primarily for himself. But there is still a long way to go.

In the beginning, the research-hungry doctor mainly used goats, sheep, and bulls as test subjects. He removes a testicle from a young animal and sews it onto an older animal. In doing so, he noticed that the vitality of the respective young animals seemed to increase.

In 1919, a year after the end of the war, Serge finally gathered enough knowledge to go public with it. He presents his findings at a Paris surgeon's congress and gives a live demonstration of his procedure.

"Men who have reached an age when physical and intellectual faculties begin to decline, when memory becomes unreliable, thinking slower, exertion higher, fatigue more rapid-men whose zest for life has been dulled or even extinguished-can reap a new source of vital activity from the creatures of the primeval forests," he proclaims. "Fortunately, one of our near relatives lives there, from whom we can procure what we need with fewer scruples."

At these words, Voronoff places a cage on the desk beside him.

"The orangutan, the chimpanzee and the gibbon!"

Immediately, some uneasiness spreads in the audience, and there are quiet whispers. The scientists don't quite trust it all yet.

"Will the man mutate into an ape after the procedure?" a reporter from the *New York Times* reports. The doctor laughs.

"Of course not!" he counters. "Let me demonstrate."

Voronoff grabs a knife and gets to work. He cuts out a testicle, already transplanted a year ago, from one of the animals and presents it to the doctors with explanatory words. The initial skepticism gradually gives way to approval, and the doctor decides to transfer the transplantation to humans.

And so, on July 12, 1920, he implanted a monkey testicle in the scrotum of a 74-year-old man for the first time. The question rightly arises here as to why he does not use human testicles for the procedure. Wouldn't these work just as well? The short answer is: yes. For Voronoff's purposes, human crown jewels would work as well. Initially, he even uses some from newly executed prisoners. However, since the logistical effort is too great for him and no one can be found who is willing to provide one of his functioning testicles, Voronoff switches to chimpanzee testicles without much hesitation.

To supply these to the human body, the doctor first cuts them into quarters like an apple. He then sews them onto his patient's testicles by cutting open the testicular capsule. This creates contact with the inner surface of the testicle, the tissue that he then sutures to the tissue of the animal testicle. In this way, he hopes that the foreign tissue will be supplied with blood because he knows that only tissue that is connected to the human bloodstream can achieve the desired effect.

After the operation, the 74-year-old man is doing well - he complains neither of pain nor any other side effects. Serge takes this as an opportunity to inspire future patients with flowery descriptions. For example, the monkey testicles are said to restore energy and help achieve beauty and "manhood." In addition, they supposedly make one smarter, faster and are even said to be able to cure schizophrenia.

At the time, he doesn't know that the old man is not feeling bad, but he is not better either; his condition remains virtually unchanged. This is because the transplanted testicular pieces have not grown and do not allow their own production of testosterone. Moreover, the concentration of testosterone in the tissue of the testicles is too low for it to have any effect on the body. Thus, Serge's procedure is kept alive by the placebo effect.

Three years after the successful transplantation, the doctor is able to convince more than 700 scientists of his new method at the International Congress of Surgeons in London. During the lecture, he also presents his colleagues with a before-and-after example of a teenager named Jean G. The picture on the left shows a black-and-white photograph of a short-haired boy with a round face. Although the caption dubs him "14 years old," his facial features resemble those of a 3-year-old. The image on the right shows a young man with neatly parted hair and more angular facial features. According to the caption, this is Jean, one year after the operation.

Voronoff shows another example on the basis of the 73-year-old M. Georges Behr. On the left, the dog eyes of an old man with bags under his eyes, a sunken face, and a half-bald head look into the camera. The gray hair to the sides is disheveled, and his dark upper lip mustache stands out clearly against the white three-day beard. The man in the right picture, on the other hand, looks like a changed man. Although there are still deep circles under his eyes, the skin of his face appears more flawless overall. His face has become a bit fuller, the stubble has been shaved off, and the hair above his ears is neat. Do these photographs prove that contrary to current findings, Serge's treatment is bearing fruit after all? Probably not. Although the pictures have an impressive effect on scientists, it must be assumed that they are merely fakes for advertising purposes. Advertising purposes, which rapidly increase the demand for transplantation in society.

In the 1920s, the operation becomes one of the most sought-after medical procedures. Millionaires from all over the world want to book an appointment with Voronoff, who continues to expand his business model. For example, he not only sews the testicles of his patients' genitals but now and then, he also sews their thighs. There, the muscles are perfused enough to be connected to the bloodstream.

Since women will soon want to have their own rejuvenation treatment with him, Serge includes the implantation of monkey ovaries, or ovaries, in his services. He even experiments with performing the procedure in reverse: he inserts a human ovary into a female monkey and wants to fertilize it with human sperm. The latter, however, fails.

In 1922, a 76-year-old man named Arthur Evelyn Liardet tells the *New York Times* that Voronoff's transplant had restored him to vitality, his wrinkles had disappeared, and his hair had grown back.

"Feel this," he says to the reporter, showing him his upper arms. "Those biceps are the envy of every 30-year-old man."

As much as young men envy his muscles, Liardet is dead two years after the procedure. While no subsequent complications from the surgery can be found, doubts are beginning to surface as to whether the Paris doctor's treatment was even worth it. After all, one was promised a long life from the monkey testicle transplant. So how can it be that the old man dies just two years later? Is it merely an isolated case? Or is there more to it than that?

Despite all this, Voronoff's discovery is gaining such notoriety that even the famous painter Pablo Picasso is said to have had an operation. Whether this is true or not is not known. However, it is a fact that at the end of the 1920s, there were no less than 3000 operations performed, 1000 of which were carried out by Voronoff himself. The handsome price of 10,000 gold francs per operation enabled Voronoff to become wealthy - at that time, the sum was equivalent to the annual salary of a chorus member at the Paris Opera. Together with his third wife, the New York oil heiress Evelyn, he occupies an entire hotel floor on the Avenue des Champs Èlysées and employs his own butlers, secretaries, drivers, and maids.

Although the high influx of patients brings the doctor a lot of money, it also poses a problem. Because of the increasing demand, the available resources are gradually becoming scarce.

The doctor, therefore, opens a monkey farm in his villa on the Italian Riviera. Located not far from the French border, the white stone building has two floors and an attic with a pitched roof and is surrounded by all kinds of trees, shrubs, and palm trees. The property is run by an animal keeper who used to work as a circus tamer. He takes care of the hundreds of chimpanzees crammed into small cages.

With all the hype surrounding him, Serge is concerned about one thing above all: as bizarre as his experiments may seem to some, he is careful not to lose his high standing within the medical world. He, therefore, accepts an invitation to the United States only on condition that he does not become a "circus act" there. Especially at the beginning of his research, he had often been regarded as a charlatan and is saddened by the humiliation he has been subjected to.

Serge Voronoff must also painfully experience firsthand that the fall is at least as fast as the rise. After 15 years of transplanting monkey testicles, Dutch scientists succeeded in isolating testosterone for the first time in 1935. What at first looked like a confirmation of Voronoff's theory quickly turned into its downfall. Although the latest results confirm the general assumption that sexual gonads produce an important substance, they also reveal that injections or transplants have no effect on the body. They do not make you younger or stronger or bring back a lack of puberty. At the same time, Voronoff's patients also notice that nothing has changed in their lives. The desired rejuvenation effect does not occur, and they continue to age normally. Some of them even die a short time after the transplant.

Voronoff now has two options to remain active as a scientist: Either he admits to himself that the data contradict his hypothesis, or he ignores the facts and acts like a businessman.

The doctor chooses option two and begins to embellish the alleged effects of his treatment more and more. For example, his patients can supposedly live up to 150 years if they undergo monkey testicle transplants with him.

To stay in the conversation, he continues his experiment around ovarian transplantation and subsequent fertilization in female monkeys. Since this continues not to work, Voronoff tries in his desperation to create a "super sheep," which, according to his ideas, should remain eternally young - also without success.

The further the doctor's career declines, the more hastily he tries to draw attention to himself with further experiments. However, this leads in the opposite direction. Instead of acknowledging his research as he had once done and showing enthusiasm, Voronoff's colleagues became increasingly skeptical of him. By the early 1940s at the latest, the doctor is publicly labeled a fraud.

But why did it take so long to find out that the monkey testicle cure did not work? Shouldn't they have figured it out sooner when the desired effect on the patients failed to materialize? The reason for this is the state of medical knowledge at that time, which was mainly based on experimental research. In the 1920s, doctors had not yet succeeded in isolating testosterone from the human body. It is therefore not possible to control, for example, based on blood samples, whether the hormone level increases or remains the same after transplantation. The driving force, in this case, remains the placebo effect. Voronoff's patients believed so strongly in the results promised to them that the physical reaction was due to their expectations.

On September 03, 1951, Voronoff died in the Swiss city of Lausanne at the age of 85 after falling in the bathtub. At the end of his life, he was left with a considerable fortune, but he was unable to regain his scientific reputation. Only a few newspapers reported on his death. And those that did write about the physician made fun of him. Despite his numerous medical breakthroughs, such as skin grafting, Voronoff is known only as the man who implanted monkey testicles into his patients - a title that still endures.

Nonetheless, his findings on mammalian sexual gonads are considered an important element of modern biology, endocrinology, as well as hormone replacement therapy. In 1999, some researchers even wanted to blame Voronoff's interventions for the origin of HIV transmission. It is now known that the virus found its way from chimpanzees to humans around 1908 in Cameroon. However, not via testicular transplantation, but presumably due to the consumption of the primates.

Not far from Voronoff Castle, as the doctor's villa is called, a wooden cage symbolizing the suffering of the animals is erected on the rocks. In the center of the cage stands a statue of a brown chimpanzee gazing with a frown at the crystal blue waters of the Ligurian Sea.

> *CHEATING AND BEING CHEATED,*
> *NOTHING IS MORE ORDINARY ON THIS*
> *PLANET.*

- Johann Gottfried Seume (1763–1810),
German writer and poet -

CHAPTER 2

MISS UNKNOWN

Russia, Ekaterinburg, night from July 16-17, 1918

The 17-year-old had fallen into a fitful sleep about two hours ago when the personal physician suddenly enters the family's chamber and shoos them all out of their beds. He says there is unrest in the city, and they must immediately hide in the basement of the house. The guards fear that there will be a gunfight that summer night. The young girl looks into the fear-filled eyes of her mother, who struggles for composure. But the woman, true to her nature, quickly regains her composure and orders her children to follow the instructions of the personal physician. Unlike her mother now, the 17-year-old can still see the concern on her father's face. Hastily, the family members, along with their servants and the little King Charles Spaniel "Jemmy," make their way to the basement of the building. Their guards lead them to an empty room. The mother-of-five complains to the commander and demands that he at least allow them two chairs. The commander sighs in annoyance but then orders one of his subordinates to fetch two seats from the upper floor. The exhausted mother sits on one of the chairs; her sick 14-year-old son sits on the other. "Jemmy" lies down on the cold floor and snuggles up to the boy's feet. The air in the small room is filled with the tension of the family and their servants facing their armed overseers. The commander asks them to line up in two rows.

There were rumors in Moscow that they had managed to escape. A photo should now prove that they are still in captivity. Uncertain, they all line up in two rows as requested. They do not speak a word. The father nods encouragingly to his 17-year-old daughter. "Everything will be all right," he probably wants to signal to her, but his furrowed brow and compressed lips do not make his encouragement seem sincere. The young girl senses that he is afraid. She sees her mother reach for her sick son's hand out of the corner of her eye. Was she sobbing? The 17-year-old thinks she sees her mother's body trembling. The girl feels a lump in her throat, cutting off her breath. She now also reaches for the hand of her 19-year-old sister, who is standing stiffly beside her. Wordlessly, the commander turns to the wooden door and pushes down the handle. But instead of the expected photographer, a firing squad enters the room. A short cry of horror escapes the mother. The other doomed men freeze, eyes wide with shock. "The government has decided that you and your family should be executed," the commander opens to the father of the family in a cool, calm voice, raising his gun. "What?!" is the last word from Russia's once most important man before the commander raises his gun, aims at the latter's heart, and fires a shot. Fatally shot, the family man collapses. Even before the others realize what has happened, the men of the firing squad begin to aim at the person the commander had previously assigned to them. The killers are to aim directly at the heart of their victim to avoid a bloodbath. One cartridge after another whizzes through the air, accompanied by deafening bangs. Even "Jemmy" is hit by a fatal shot. But the commander's plan does not work. The brutal mass murder lasts twenty minutes until all the victims have taken what seems to be their last breath. When the family and its servants were initially still in custody at the Alexander Palace, the chambermaid Anna Demidova had worked with the family's daughters to sew smaller valuables and expensive jewelry into their bodices and pillows. The jewelry and a pillow, which the chambermaid tried to use to ward off the bullets, now act like a bulletproof vest, making it impossible for the assassins to kill their victims with just one shot. In short order, the men take up their bayonets and stab the defenseless survivors, who have nothing to oppose their attackers.

Weimar Republic, Berlin, on the evening of February 17, 1920

A sunny, almost spring-like Tuesday is drawing to a close. Near Potsdamer Platz, a group of protective police patrols the area. One of the men spots a woman walking along on what is now the Bendler Bridge. He pays no further attention to her and turns back to his colleagues, who are engrossed in a conversation.

But the policeman doesn't have much to contribute to the conversation, so his gaze wanders back over to the bridge. The woman stands on the railing and looks down at the canal. Suddenly she decisively swings herself over the railing. Her heels are the only thing holding her to the edge of the bridge. Turning her arms backward, she holds on to the railing.

The policeman's shout breaks the evening's silence: "Don't do that! The woman looks up briefly and glances in the direction from which she suspects the admonition is coming. But her decision is made; no one can stop her now. Even as she plunges toward the water's surface, the protective policeman sprints off.

Arriving at the bank of the canal, the man does not hesitate for a second, jumps into the cold water, and swims to the woman. Although it takes him only a few moments to reach her, she is already in danger of drowning. Again and again, her head dives underwater; she flails her arms wildly. He courageously reaches under her left armpit from behind, takes her, and swims back to the safe shore.

The other police officers are already waiting for them there. The men lose no time and take the rescued woman to a nearby clinic.

The young woman appears confused to the doctor on duty and the hospital nurses. First, due to the threat of hypothermia, she is taken out of her deeply wet robe and given dry and warm clothes. While changing her clothes, the nurse notices some scars on the slender patient's body. She also notices that the woman, who seems confused, no longer seems to have any incisors. But no matter how reassuringly the nurse talks to her patient and cares for her, not a word escapes the young woman's lips during her entire stay in the hospital. After the unknown woman has been nursed back to health by the hospital staff and is physically better, the doctor transfers her to the Dalldorf mental hospital, today's Karl Bonhoeffer Mental Hospital.

The psychiatrist has no idea who he is dealing with. He sits broodingly across from the new addition to the clinic at his desk. What is her name? Where is she from? What does she do for a living? Why did she want to take her own life? He has questions upon questions, but he has no answers to expect from his patient. In addition to her physically desolate condition, she also makes a psychologically battered impression on the physician. Sighing, he reaches for his fountain pen and scribbles in the name box of the patient's file: "Miss Unknown.

Perhaps, some clinic employees suspect, she is one of the many poor women from the hinterland who come to Berlin after the end of the First World War to build a better life for themselves here. Not infrequently, however, the plan goes awry, and the women have to prostitute themselves or commit petty racketeering to get by. No one can blame them if they suffer a mental breakdown under these circumstances.

There are different accounts of how the following incident came about. Some report that a Russian couple shows a photo to the unknown person; others tell that a nurse in Dalldorf or a fellow patient set the ball rolling when they leafed through a tabloid newspaper. However it happened, one person believes he recognizes the unknown patient in a picture of Tsar Nicholas II, his wife, and their children, who still refuses to reveal her identity almost two years after her suicide attempt.

One summer night in July 1918, the Russian tsar's family had been brutally executed by a firing squad in the basement of a house in Yekaterinburg, fenced in by man-sized boards and guarded by heavily armed Bolsheviks, as part of the revolution. A crime that shook the world. Perhaps that is why the rumor persists that one of the tsar's daughters may have survived the slaughter. After all, the Bolshevists had buried the bodies of the tsar's family and their servants in a secret place, and no one knows who really lost their lives on that night of blood.

It is October 23, 1921, when someone confronts the unknown patient with the alleged striking resemblance to one of the children of Nicholas II. The woman with full lips and big eyes between a somewhat bulbous nose looks at the photo for a few seconds. Then she raises her eyes and says in a chest tone of conviction, "Yes. It's true. I am the Grand Duchess Anastasia Nikolaevna Romanova."

News that the youngest daughter of the tsar survived the Yekaterinburg bloodbath and is now in the Dalldorf mental hospital slips over the walls of the facility and spreads to the public. The press pounces on the story of Anastasia, who was believed dead. The population is divided. In particular, some Russian émigrés who fled Russia for Germany before the violent revolution clings to the idea that a member of the tsar's family is still alive. The scars on her body and the missing incisors, some are sure, testify to the crime committed against the young woman by the Bolshevists. Others, however, believe that "Miss Unknown" is an impostor - after all, the woman, who looks more like she is in her mid- than early twenties, bears no resemblance at all to the 17-year-old tsar's daughter Anastasia depicted in the photographs.

The Dalldorfer patient, who from now on wants to be addressed only as "Imperial Highness," now reveals more and more details about her past and her escape to Berlin. When the bodies of her parents and siblings were taken away on that night of bloodshed, she was seriously injured but still alive. Alexander Tchaikovsky - a loyal subject and a remorseful guard - had noticed that. With the surviving tsar's daughter, the man escaped to Romania's capital, Bucharest. Once there, they would have married quite soon. But the marriage was short-lived. One day, Tchaikovsky was shot dead on the streets of Bucharest. A brother of the dead man, Anastasia's brother-in-law, then accompanied the widow to Germany. Here the young woman wanted to seek refuge with her aunt, Princess Heinrich of Prussia. But this did not work out; she does not mention the reasons for this. Her fragmentary story ends with the fact that she wandered the streets of Berlin penniless without her brother-in-law and finally, out of sheer desperation, wanted to take her own life in the Berlin Landwehrkanal.

But why had the Dalldorfer patient concealed her true identity for so long? The woman also has a plausible answer to that: she didn't feel safe at first but gradually gained confidence. And now that someone recognized her from the photo of the tsar's family, she summoned up all her courage and finally told her story.

Above all, a large part of the Russian nobility believes the woman. They hope that the Romanova family will one day regain the Russian throne. The fact that the tsar's daughter does not speak a word of Russian is further proof for all the doubters. But the Russian nobility has an explanation for the circumstance: the young woman has been severely traumatized by the brutal act of the Bolshevists and has therefore suppressed her mother tongue. This also explains other gaps in the Romanova daughter's knowledge about the tsar's family, they believe.

Numerous doctors examine the alleged imperial highness. Among them was the famous psychiatrist Karl Bonhoeffer, who examined the woman in 1926. At the end of his exploration, however, even he remained undecided as to whether he was dealing with the survivor of the mass murder of the tsar's family.

Meanwhile, under the leadership of the Baltic Baron von Kleist, the expelled Russian nobility obtains the immediate release of the tsar's daughter from the Dalldorf insane asylum. The fact that, among others, the mother of Tsar Nicholas II, his youngest sister, the French teacher of the tsar's children, and the nanny reject the woman who believes to be Grand Duchess Anastasia cannot deter her supporters.

Nor when a woman named Doris Wingender reports to the Berlin police in 1927, claiming to know "Miss Unknown." While leafing through a magazine, Ms. Wingender discovered the illustrated article about the alleged daughter of the tsar. After only a few seconds of looking at the pictures, she was quite sure:

the photo shows the former tenant of her parents. The young woman's name is Franziska Czenstkowski. In 1919 and early 1920, she lived in a small apartment in her parents' apartment building at Neue Hochstraße 17 in the working-class district of Wedding. But one day, Franziska disappeared without a trace and was reported missing to the police in March 1920.

The police investigate and contact the brother and sister of the missing woman. They present the relatives with photos of the alleged tsar's daughter. The siblings leave no doubt that the woman pictured is their missing sister Franziska. But this fact is largely ignored by the public. The fascination with the story of the surviving Grand Duchess Anastasia is too great.

On the other hand, the latter is getting a little out of touch with Europe - she fears she will be exposed after Doris Wingender has talked to the police. On a ship, the 32-year-old sets off for America in 1928. Once there, she meets wealthy patrons who provide her with a good living as the supposed daughter of the tsar, Anastasia.

But the young woman's mental state experiences a seemingly bottomless low after the heady high. She is committed to an American mental institution after dancing naked on a rooftop and kicking one of her budgies to death. Only a short time later, the authorities expel the sick woman from the country. Anna Anderson, as the woman now prefers to be called, returns to Germany. Once there, however, her treatment must continue. She is sent to a mental hospital in Hanover. Her release follows in 1932.

"Miss Unknown" sticks to her story, despite all adversities. In 1938, she even goes to court and fights for recognition. With the confirmation of her identity, she would also be the rightful heiress to the assets of the slain tsar's family - provided that the lost treasure should one day reappear. Gold, jewelry, and precious stones belonging to Europe's once richest ruler would be worth around 55 billion euros today. With the start of World War II, however, the court halted the proceedings for the time being. The country now has other problems to contend with.

From then on, Anderson traveled through Germany; she found shelter with her patrons. An unsteady life without a real home. It was not until 1947 that the now 51-year-old took refuge in an inconspicuous cottage in the Black Forest. She lived there, lonely and withdrawn, in the small building whose walls and ceilings she painted unevenly and streaky with blood-red paint. Throughout the house, which she shares with 60 cats and 4 dogs, disorder and chaos rule.

As affectionate as she is with her animals, she is merciless to the people who care for them. She is said to have bullied the volunteers with sadistic glee.

It is 1951 when medical progress allows Anna Anderson to undergo a blood test at Heidelberg University Hospital. The doctors intend to detect hereditary carriers of hemophilia, from which Anastasia's murdered brother Alexei had suffered since birth. But the blood test does not bring the desired breakthrough. The doctors cannot prove but also exclude any carriers of the disease.

A few years later, a new trial is underway in Hamburg for the recognition of Anna Anderson as Grand Duchess Anastasia. A long, drawn-out trial. Anderson refuses to appear in court in person. And so, in February 1967, the judge hands down his verdict in the absence of the plaintiff: Anna Anderson is not recognized as the tsar's daughter Anastasia and the rightful heiress of the tsar's lost treasure. The supporters of the alleged Grand Duchess Anastasia slink out of the back entrance of the court - so embarrassed are they for the court's finding. Meanwhile, the press turns to a new sensation. An elderly lady in a brown coat appears in the court corridor, shouting loudly: "The verdict is correct! Because I am the real Anastasia!".

After the fiasco in court, things are getting worse for 72-year-old Anna Anderson in Germany. It is the year 1968 when she turns her back on the Black Forest and moves to the USA again. There she meets John Eacott Manahan, a historian, and millionaire 20 years her junior. The man firmly believes that he has before him the surviving daughter of the Tsar, Anastasia. The historian marries his newfound acquaintance to legalize the woman's stay in the US.

The couple lives in seclusion in Charlottesville in the US state of Virginia. Here, the alleged daughter of the czar no longer has any volunteers. John Manahan now takes their place. He, too, is said to have been at the mercy of the old woman's harassment.

Only a short time after the newlyweds had moved into their house, the fire department has to move in and clean up the estate. The Manahans can no longer keep up with the care of their approximately 100 cats and 29 dogs. The property is in danger of drowning in animal feces. Until their deaths, the couple lives a secluded and lonely life. Only their numerous pets keep them company in their self-imposed exile.

On February 17, 1970, exactly 50 years after " Miss Unknown " was rescued from the Berlin Landwehr Canal, the Federal Court of Justice upholds the first verdict of the Hanseatic Court from 1967. However, this does not stop her husband Manahan from believing in his wife's story and supporting her until his death in 1990.

On February 12, 1984, Anna Anderson-Manahan also passes away at the age of 87 after a long, serious illness. The body's cremation occurs on the very day of her death. The urn is sent to Germany. In June 1984, the vessel is lowered into the ground in the Orthodox section of the Walburgiskapelle Seeon cemetery in Bavaria. Her patrons, the family of the Dukes of Leuchtenberg, are also buried here.

Seven years after the death of the alleged tsar's daughter, who swore stone and stone to be the Grand Duchess Anastasia until her passing, the mortal remains of Tsar Nicholas II, his wife, and three of their daughters are discovered near Ekaterinburg in 1991. After detailed investigations, it is determined that the skeleton of the tsar's son Alexei is missing. Nor can the remains of any of the daughters be found. Is Anastasia possibly missing? Can the story of Anna Anderson, who appears confused, be true after all? The last doubts remain.

Two years later, British scientist Peter Gill makes a sensational discovery. The man locates a piece of small intestine that doctors removed and preserved from Anna Anderson while she was alive in a hospital. With the evidence from the hospital and a sample from Prince Philip, husband of England's Queen Elizabeth II, the scientist manages to solve the mystery of "Miss Unknown." Prince Philip was a great-nephew of the murdered Tsarina Alexandra, wife of Nicholas II, so the DNA of the English prince should be similar to that of Anna Anderson. But the result is negative. Peter Gill provides scientific proof: Anna Anderson is not Grand Duchess Anastasia.

In 1998, the remains of the Romanov family were buried in a festive ceremony in the Peter and Paul Cathedral in St. Petersburg. It was not until 9 years later, in 2007, that Russian archaeologists also discovered the remains of the heir to the throne Alexei and another daughter of the tsar in a birch forest in the Urals. After several examinations, it is soon clear that the last female skeleton is Maria Romanov. Scientists can now confirm beyond any doubt that among the first human bones found were the remains of Anastasia. The young girl, just like her family members and servants, was brutally murdered by the Bolshevists that summer night. The story of a successful escape - obviously a fairy tale.

After all investigations, the tsar's son Alexei and his sister Maria are reunited with their dead family members in the Peter and Paul Cathedral in St. Petersburg. The Orthodox "Cathedral on the Blood" has stood on the former site of the murder house since 2003. Even today, the magnificent church is intended to remind people of the sad fate of the Romanovs.

But who was Anna Anderson, really? Even years after her death, historians and scientists are still puzzled by the question. They set out in search of clues to finally unravel the mystery of "Miss Unknown." In southern Germany, a doctor draws blood from a relative of Franziska Czenstkowski, a farm worker who disappeared in 1920. The man is a grandson of Gertrud, a sister of Franziska. At the end of the elaborate examinations, it is clear that the man's mitochondrial DNA is identical to that of his great-aunt Franziska. Mitochondria are organelles and are considered the "powerhouse of the cell." Unlike DNA, which is found in the cell nucleus, mitochondrial DNA contains only genes from the mother of the individual. Scientists now have unequivocal proof: Anna Anderson, alias Grand Duchess Anastasia, was, in fact, the agricultural worker Franziska Czenstkowski. Like a jigsaw puzzle, one piece now fits into the next to form a complete picture.

Franziska was born in West Prussia on December 22, 1896. Her parents were Anton, a tenant farmer, and his wife, Marianne. The farmer's daughter lived with her family in the Kashubian region, which at that time belonged to the German Reich, in Pomerelia in Poland. Franziska grows up in poor circumstances. The family's few possessions also fall victim to their father, Anton's alcoholism.

Franziska stands out among her five siblings. The girl reads a lot and announces early on that she does not want to stay in her home village. "I have to leave here," she says again and again. The farmer's daughter also stands out among her peers. Unlike her peers, she always dresses smartly - as well as the family's few financial resources allow. In addition to fancy dresses, Franziska always wears little hats and slips decorative gloves over her hands.

It is 1912 when her father, Anton, dies. Franziska now has nothing left in her home village. The 16-year-old turns her back on her homeland. She looks for a better life in Berlin, the metropolis of the German Empire. At first, she finds a job there as a maid. But after World War I breaks out in Europe in 1914, Franziska is conscripted into service. She has to work in a munitions factory. In 1916, a devastating accident occurs there. A live grenade accidentally falls out of the 19-year-old's hand, causing the explosive projectile to detonate. The detonation kills Franziska's colleague before her eyes. On the other hand, the young woman sustains only minor injuries in the accident but suffers a shock. The explosion also explains the numerous scars on the woman's body.

From then on, she makes an absent and confused impression on the other factory employees. Franziska is sent to a mental hospital in Neuruppin. For the first time, the symptoms that would accompany her throughout the rest of her life became apparent. For days, the 19-year-old hid in her bed. She is apathetic and does not respond to doctors and nurses. The young woman sometimes seems to have forgotten who she is, according to the doctors treating her. In October 1917, Franziska was allowed to leave the mental hospital. In the discharge book of the institution, the doctors note that the patient's condition had "improved." There is no mention of a cure at the time of her release.

Franziska wandered the streets of Berlin until she decided to end her young life on that February night in 1920.

Later, it also turns out what happened to her incisors. Allegedly, the woman lost them to the blow of a rifle butt on the night her family was murdered - in reality, however, doctors had removed parts of her teeth for reasons that have not been disclosed in the Dalldorf mental hospital.

Numerous authors dealt with the story of Franziska Czenstkowski alias Anna Anderson; various journalists wrote articles about the woman. And the film world was also inspired by the mystery of the allegedly surviving daughter of the czar. In February 1957, the film drama "Anastasia," starring the famous Swedish actress Ingrid Bergmann as the Grand Duchess, premiered in Germany. The US film production company "20th Century Fox" based its lovingly designed and lavishly produced animated film "Anastasia" on the events surrounding Anna Anderson, among other things. After the film was released in 1997, the makers were able to enjoy various awards - among others, "Anastasia" was also nominated for an Oscar in 1998 in the categories "Best Music" and "Best Song."

To this day, however, it is not clear whether "Miss Unknown" suffered from a mental illness and actually believed she was the tsar's daughter Anastasia Nikolayevna Romanova, or whether she was an impostor who deliberately tried to deceive her fellow human beings. Just an impostor - that, most people believe, she undoubtedly was. But one thing is also certain: whether or not Franziska Czenstkowski knew about her true origins, throughout her life, the woman was a deeply unhappy person who never really benefited from the fairy tale of being Grand Duchess Anastasia.

I ADMONISH YOU, ICARUS, TO KEEP YOURSELF ON A MIDDLE COURSE, LEST, IF YOU GO TOO LOW, THE WAVES WEIGH DOWN THE FEATHERS, AND IF YOU FLY TOO HIGH, THE FIRE SCORCH THEM. FLY BETWEEN THE TWO.

- Publius Ovidius Naso (43 v. Chr.-17 n. Chr.)
Roman epic poet -

CHAPTER 3

HIGH ABOVE

At Amsterdam's Schiphol Airport, a Boeing 737 of the budget airline "Corendon Airlines" sparkles under the glistening sun under a bright blue sky. 101 passengers are waiting for the experienced captain to take the aircraft into the sky and fly them safely to the Turkish capital Ankara. While the flight attendants help the travelers stow their hand luggage and familiarize them with the necessary safety precautions, the pilot walks around his plane on the tarmac. Some of the passengers watch the man from the oval windows. Over his black jacket, with the gold stripes on the sleeve, a neon yellow high-visibility vest flutters in the wind. He wears a white pilot's cap with a black visor on his head. He protects his eyes from the bright sunlight with tinted glasses. The Swede inspects the turbines, checks the tire pressure, and examines the wings. Only when the stately man with the wild, somewhat gray curls and the winning smile is satisfied with the condition of his aircraft does he join his co-pilot in the cockpit and go through the pre-takeoff checklist with him. His colleagues appreciate the pilot for his calm, level-headed nature. Even in the most stressful and even dicey situations, the pilot radiates an unshakable calm. But when two policemen approach the big man, who is otherwise unperturbed by anything or anyone, and politely ask him to show them his pilot's license, beads of sweat appear on the pilot's forehead. He reaches into the inside pocket of his jacket. With shaky fingers, he pulls out the requested piece of paper and hands it to one of the officers. While the policeman carefully studies the document with his colleague, the pilot turns his head and casts a wistful glance over his shoulder at the narrow-body aircraft ready for takeoff. He knew that this moment would come one day.

Thomas Salme was born in Stockholm, Sweden on February 18, 1969. His father is a programmer, and his mother takes care of the housework and lovingly looks after her only son. The small family lives in Jordbro - a village in the municipality of Haninge, about 20 kilometers from Stockholm.

The boy with the wild, blond mane and steel-blue eyes discovered his love of aviation at an early age. On weekends, armed with a photo camera, father and son set off for Stockholm's Arlanda Airport - where they watch the planes take off and land. With every plane that thunders overhead, the 8-year-old puts his head back. Wide-eyed and open-mouthed in wonder, Thomas gazes up at the sky and admiringly follows the flight path of the majestic-looking aircraft. But the boy inherited his love of aviation from his father and his passion for photography. The only child takes countless pictures of planes taking off and landing. The boy glues the most beautiful photos into a photo album.

Thomas is 10 years old when he sits in an airplane as a passenger for the first time. The family is on a vacation trip to Madeira. The boy presses his nose against the small oval window next to his seat. The freedom above the clouds seems limitless to him. Now, at the latest, the boy is certain: he wants to become a pilot.

But first, the Swede goes through a regular school career and graduates from a technical high school at the age of 19. The Salme family does not have any great wealth. But the couple manages to put aside $16500 for their son. The young man decides to use it to pave the way for his big dream. At a flight school near Stockholm, he trained as a private pilot for single-engine aircraft with an instrument flight license - an integral part of possibly obtaining a pilot's license for commercial aircraft at a later date. Instrument flying, also called blind flying, is done only with the help of the flight instruments on board the aircraft.

The Swede's passion for flying is also reflected in the exams: Thomas Salme passes all the tests as the best in the course.

Full of ambition and self-confidence, the 22-year-old then applies for a place at the renowned SAS Flight Academy. Here he wants to obtain his pilot's license to fly commercial aircraft and fulfill his lifelong dream: Finally flying one of the big passenger jets himself. But Thomas is faced with an almost insoluble problem. The Second Gulf War is raging in the Middle East. The whole world is struggling with the effects - some more, others less. After the oil price skyrockets following the outbreak of the war, the market gradually regulates itself when it is determined that a number of producers will be able to increase their production quotas, thus securing global oil supplies. In February 1991, the oil price is even lower than before the outbreak of the Second Gulf War. Soon, the aviation industry also feels the effects of cheap oil. Air routes are discontinued to counter the financial losses. Many people employed in the aviation industry lose their jobs. The "SAS Flight Academy" is also not spared the effects of the crisis. They have to cut back support for their protégés and are canceling the scholarship program. Anyone who now decides to become a professional pilot is forced to pay for the demanding and expensive training out of their own pocket. As much as Thomas' parents want to help him fulfill his dream, they can't afford their son's training. But the 22-year-old Swede doesn't want to give up just yet. The young man makes countless loan requests to various banks. But they all refuse to grant Salme a loan - the financial institutions justify their decision by saying that the career prospects as a professional pilot are too bad.

Thomas is frustrated. He can't believe that as the best student at the flight school, his big dream should be denied to him. After several rejections for a loan, the young man realizes that it is futile. He is forced to change his career. Disgruntled, Salme gets a job as an audio technician at a health insurance company. He doesn't enjoy his job but needs the pay to make a living. After all, you can't pay bills by just dreaming. But hardly a day goes by when the injustice he suffers eats further and further into his soul like a tumor.

But giving up is not an option for the ambitious Swede. He doggedly sticks to his plan. There must be a way to fulfill his desire for freedom above the clouds in the cockpit of a passenger plane. His friendship with a young man who works as a technician at the SAS Flight Academy actually opens the first door to his great dream. The Swede's friend knows how urgent Salme's desire is to become a professional pilot. To cheer him up a bit, the technician smuggles him into the pilot academy at night. A risky favor: If another employee were to catch on to the nighttime excursions, the technician would be out of a job. But perhaps the two young men are still too clueless to grasp the implications of this venture. Salme's friend probably has no idea what path he is actually paving for his buddy.

The technician grants his friend forbidden access to the high-security wing of the pilot academy. This is where the flight simulators are located, where future professional pilots learn to fly on the ground and train how to behave in dangerous situations.

Over the next year and a half, Salme will practice in one of the flight simulators about 20 times for two to three hours each time. While he flies virtually around the world, he forgets everything else around him.

During his first attempts at flying, he has to accept a few crash landings. But this does not discourage the young Swede. After each crash, the Swede analyzes the mistake he made that caused the cockpit of the aircraft to bore into the virtual ground. He continues to train doggedly, trying out the controls of different aircraft models. He soon discovers that he is particularly comfortable operating a Boeing 737-300. The function and meaning of the numerous instruments become apparent to the young man as if by magic.

With each training session, Salme gains self-confidence. Unfavorable weather conditions or difficult approaches to tricky runways: The young man masters all the challenges presented to him by the flight simulator.

Thomas believes he is now ready. He makes himself a flight permit out of ordinary copy paper, for which he doesn't even go to any great lengths. Supposedly, the license was issued in Sweden, as the made-up logo on the paper indicates. Salme doesn't even bother to shrink-wrap the fake document or put stamps of any kind on it. He writes a cover letter and attaches his fictitious flight permit to it. The 28-year-old addressed the application letter to "Air One" in Rome, Italy, and took the large envelope to the post office without much hope of a reply. Later, he will say that the whole action was just a " stupid" idea.

It takes a few weeks before Salme has mail in his mailbox from the low-cost airline, which mainly offers domestic flights to Pisa or Milan. Thomas assumes he knows what the airline's letter says when he opens the envelope with trembling fingers. He stares in disbelief at the written lines. The young man cannot believe what he is reading. In his hands, Salme holds the official invitation to test fly in a flight simulator - the first step toward being hired.

The Swede sets off for Italy in June 1997, full of confidence. If there's one thing he knows how to do, it's operate a flight simulator. He sits in the simulator for four hours with the airline's examiner. None of the tasks posed presents him with any difficulties. Even an emergency landing with the engines out of action doesn't faze Salme. The examiner is impressed by the candidate's flying skills. Thomas has mastered the selection process with flying colors. At the end of the virtual flight, the Italian takes a cursory glance at Salme's fake commercial pilot's license. Nevertheless, the young Swede holds his breath for a brief moment until the examiner welcomes him as a new colleague with a handshake.

Salme will never forget his first flight as a co-pilot in a passenger jet. He is not afraid of his baptism of fire. Pushing up on the thrust levers for the first time and feeling the nose of the aircraft, which weighs tons, stretch toward the sky and the engine lose traction; watching the sunrise at 10,000 meters for the first time - an awe-inspiring experience for the Swede. In his wildest dreams, the captain cannot imagine an impostor sitting next to him in the cockpit. Despite his first flight, the co-pilot makes a confident and balanced impression on the experienced professional pilot. Of course, Salme's first flights do not go smoothly. Thomas makes minor mistakes - but no major blunders. The captain knows that this is not unusual. Co-pilots are not perfect.

Every six months, the young Swede has to pass an internationally prescribed test in the flight simulator - an easy task for him. Every time he has to present his poorly forged flight permit and no one notices the fraud, Salme's self-confidence grows a bit more. He meticulously has the accumulated flying hours documented in his logbook.

The captains are extremely satisfied with the performance of the likable Swede, whom all his colleagues appreciate for his level-headed and friendly manner. Salme lives his lie. He feels like a real pilot. Thomas quickly pushes aside any nascent remorse about his imposture. "I'm doing a great job," he tells himself, "otherwise I would have made a serious mistake long ago. And none of the experienced captains has ever complained about my work."

No one knows anything about his secret. Family and friends believe that the young Swede found a financial way to finance his training as a professional pilot. Not even the woman at his side suspects that she is marrying a fraud.

It is 1999 when the 30-year-old is happy about his promotion to captain of "Air One." The fear that someone might notice the forgery of his pilot's license fades with each successfully completed flight. Even when gusts of wind make it difficult for him to approach the destination airport with his passenger plane and, to make matters worse, an eagle gets caught in one of his plane's engines, Salme remains calm and focused. Only when the impostor leaves the cockpit with soft knees and feels solid ground under his feet again does he realize how dicey the situation is. But the fact that he masters every challenge and always gets his passengers to their destination safely reinforces his life's lie.

In the summer of 2006, Salme joins the British low-cost airline "Jet 2". Now the impostor also flies his fully loaded planes to Germany, landing and taking off in Düsseldorf. After only ten months with Jet 2, however, the self-styled pilot successfully joins the Turkish-Dutch low-cost airline Corendon Airline.

Until that fateful March 02, 2010, when two police officers approached the captain at Schiphol Airport in the Netherlands and demanded his license, authorities had received an anonymous tip that for 13 years now, an impostor had been taking thousands of passengers through the air to their destinations in machines weighing tons. The source blabbed that he never trained as a professional pilot but only has an expired private pilot's license.

The police officers ask the Swede to accompany them. Salme does not have to think long about what to do now. Without further ado, he admits that he is not a pilot. For 13 years and 10,000 flying hours, he had been a fraud with forged documents. The officers can't believe their ears when the 41-year-old tells them his incredible story.

News of the arrested impostor spreads like wildfire, splitting people into two camps. Some think the Swede is an irresponsible fraudster who knowingly put the lives of thousands of people in the air and on the ground in unscrupulous danger. Others, however, admire Salme for his uncompromising will not to let his dream be taken away from him and see a natural aviation talent in the impostor.

In April 2013, the fake pilot, who wanted to fly high and instead crash-landed professionally, faces a Dutch court. Before the trial, Salme is tense. What punishment awaits him now? He was always confident in his flying skills and got his passengers safely to their destinations. But would a jurist, who has no idea of flying and perhaps only the possible dangers 10 kilometers above the earth in his head, also see it that way? When the chairman pronounces his verdict, Salme breathes a sigh of relief. The judge has been lenient. The Swede is fined $2250 and banned from flying for 12 months. "Perhaps," muses the judge as he hands down the sentence, "you should think about training to become a professional pilot now." But as much as Thomas Salme loves the boundless freedom above the clouds - pilot training for commercial aircraft is out of the question for the man. Then he would have to start all over again. The Swede explains his decision. The prosecutor is also impressed by Salme's flying skills. "You might think you could say that (Salme) has endangered air traffic all these years, but the fact is that he flew for 13 years without incident," the lawyer tells a newspaper.

On the other hand, a spokeswoman for the prosecutor's office is less enthusiastic about the fake pilot. She tells members of the press that the Justice Ministry wants to carefully examine the verdict against Salme and weigh whether to appeal. After all, the spokeswoman continues, the verdict is unsatisfactory for those who were on the plane with Salme as the pilot. But the appeal deadline passes without the public prosecutor's office filing a corresponding motion. As a result, the verdict becomes legally binding.

"Corendon Airline," which was the last to employ the fake pilot, is drawing consequences from the scandal. The airline is tightening its vetting process for pilots applying for employment. And the safety officers of European aviation are also taking action after it was revealed that Salme amateurishly falsified his pilot's license, and yet no one noticed. No one should take the opportunity to exploit loopholes in the aviation system again; the pilot document should be forgery-proof. Because as Salme later explained to some reporters, flight licenses in Europe are not visually uniform. This, in turn, means that an airline based in Italy, for example, does not know what a pilot's license looks like in Sweden and vice versa. Ultimately, he took advantage of this circumstance.

In 2012, Thomas Salme published his biography in Swedish with Norderstedt Publishing under the title "En bluffpilots bekännelse: Thomas Salmes 13 år i himlen" (in English: "The Confession of a Fraud Pilot: Thomas Salmes 13 years in heaven").

The aviation industry's hopes that the impostor Salme was an isolated case are dashed a few years later. William C. has been flying for "South African Airways" for 25 years. In November 2018, he sits as co-pilot in the cockpit of an Airbus A340-600 en route from Johannesburg to Frankfurt and gets caught in violent turbulence high above the Alps. Fortunately, none of the passengers or crew members are injured. Although William C. lands the aircraft safely at the destination airport alongside a responsible captain, a routine check by the airline occurs because the Airbus was traveling significantly faster than the maximum speed allowed during the turbulence. In addition to the violent air turbulence, exceeding the maximum speed also poses a risk to the aircraft's structure. Only now is it coming out: William C. has a valid commercial pilot's license, unlike Thomas Salme at the time, but not a license for airline transport pilots. According to the airline's guidelines, its co-pilots must present a commercial pilot certificate after five years of employment with South African Airways. William C. had simply issued this certificate to himself without further ado. For this reason, the man had also refused the promotions that were constantly offered to him - the risk was too great for the man that the swindle could be exposed after a detailed examination of his document.

Not much has become publicly known about the private life of fake pilot Thomas Salme. One newspaper reports that Salme is divorced; another article says that the father of two sons lives with his wife and children in Milan, Italy.

What is certain is that the now 53-year-old changed his career and made his second passion, photography, his business. The Swedish-born photographer now supplies several magazines with professionally produced fashion and sports photos.

Salme doesn't have a guilty conscience. "I'm a good, serious pilot and was level-headed even in dicey situations," he defends his lack of remorse.

THOU SHALT NOT COVET THY NEIGHBOR'S WIFE, MANSERVANT, MAIDSERVANT, OX, DONKEY, OR ANYTHING ELSE THAT THY NEIGHBOR HAS.

- The Bible / 10th Commandment -

CHAPTER 4

THE STRENGTH OF A WOMAN

The woman clutches the black leather-covered steering wheel so tightly that her knuckles bulge, and the skin on the back of her hand turns white. She feels her heart beating hard against her rib cage. Her throat is dry; there's cold sweat on her forehead. The 46-year-old adjusts the dark brown frame of a pair of large sunglasses with which she tries to hide the eye area of her narrow face. She doesn't want anyone to notice her almost unbearable tension. To make sure that nobody recognizes her, she has wrapped a dark silk scarf around her head and neck. A small headphone is plugged into her right ear. The permanent, monotonous noise develops into an ever-louder drone in her head. "He's coming toward your car now," a male voice snaps the mother of three out of her thoughts. The voice pierces from the small button in her ear. "Stay very calm. No matter what he says, don't open the door," the voice instructs her. Just a few seconds later, a tall, slender man knocks on the side window of her car. Out of the corner of her eye, the woman recognizes the person who put her in this unpleasant situation, who abused her trust and did not hesitate to destroy her family and her reputation. Anger rises up in her. She presses her full lips together and clutches the steering wheel of her BMW even tighter. There's no turning back now. She has to go through with this - for her family, for all the other women, and not least for herself. "Marie, I want to talk to you!" she hears from outside, "come on, what's going on?". To lend emphasis to his request, he shakes the door handle of the car from outside. She briefly turns her gaze to the man next to her car. He nervously runs his hand through his hair. "Now!" she hears the male voice in her ear again. With trembling hands, she presses a button, whereupon the tailgate of the car opens almost silently. As soon as the lanky man notices this, he is no longer interested in Marie or in talking to her. Nervously, he looks around the busy rest area before hurrying to the trunk of the BMW. Determined, he reaches for the large, silver aluminum trunks. Without closing the car's tailgate or taking one last look at Marie, the man moves away with long strides. In her side mirror, the 46-year-old sees him disappear with his loot behind the trailer of a 40-ton truck. Her body begins to shake as the stress of the past few days falls away from her. Now it's out of her hands. Now it's up to the plainclothes officers to bring the matter to a conclusion. Suddenly, she hears loud shouts of "On the floor! GET ON THE GROUND!". Marie feels as if her head is stuck in a giant cotton ball. With wobbly legs, she gets out of her car. Her knees threaten to give way as she walks slowly around the 40-ton truck and watches from a distance as two police officers squat on the lanky man's back. His hands are already being held together by handcuffs on his back. Another officer grabs the aluminum cases and stows them in the civilian squad car before the two officers hoist the arrested man to his feet and lead him to the car as well. Only now does Marie realize that she hasn't been breathing properly for minutes. She takes a deep breath and feels the cold air flow into her lungs. Finally, it's over.

Marie Kallmann* is born in April 1962 in the Hessian district town of Bad Homburg vor der Höhe. Her 51-year-old father is a wealthy industrialist who is married to her mother, Elisabeth* - his former secretary - on her third marriage. Four years after Marie's birth, her little brother Maximilian* is born.

Mother Elisabeth, 16 years younger than her husband Helmut*, is a down-to-earth woman despite the family's wealth. The Kallmanns, who are considered Germany's most successful business family, do not display their wealth to the outside world. The couple are quiet, unassuming people, always careful to stay out of the limelight. After all, capital does not only mean financial carefreeness but also attracts envious people, beggars, and even criminals. This was also the case in 1978 when the police were able to thwart a kidnapping of Elisabeth and her 16-year-old daughter by a gang of 14 men in broad daylight at the last minute. The men were planning to blackmail the head of the family and wanted to demand several million Deutschmarks for the women's release.

A frightening experience. From then on, Marie and Maximilian are accompanied by bodyguards, and Helmut and Elisabeth shy away from public attention even more than ever before. Even when the Kallmanns host a party, they rarely mingle with the party guests. They sit reservedly together at a table and talk quietly to each other while they enjoy the fact that the visitors are enjoying their hospitality.

Elisabeth raises the children, following her own virtues, to be self-controlled and modest.

Marie graduates from the Kaiserin-Friedrich-Gymnasium in Hesse before training as an advertising saleswoman at an agency in Frankfurt am Main from 1981 to 1983. The 21-year-old then moved to England to attend Buckingham Private University, where she successfully studied business administration. She then does an internship at Deutsche Bank AG before completing a postgraduate generalist management course at a private business school in the Swiss city of Lausanne.

During Marie's training as an advertising executive in the early 1980s, her father, Helmut, dies shortly before his 72nd birthday. The 56-year-old Elisabeth and her children inherit most of his fortune - including shares in BMW AG. But the widow does not sit back after her husband's death. While daughter Marie completes an internship at the BMW plant in Regensburg under a pseudonym, undetected by the employees, her mother works in a canteen.

Marie meets a young man at the BMW plant in Regensburg. For months, Klaus Wagner* is said to have had no idea that he was involved with the daughter of Kallmann, once Germany's most influential industrialist. In 1990, the 28-year-old marries the young engineer. In the course of their marriage, the couple has three children together.

Marie Wagner lives as her mother taught her: modestly and reservedly. The public hardly notices her, and she wants to keep it that way. She, therefore, does not give interviews to members of the press.

The slender woman, who wears her blonde hair in a fashionable short cut, usually dresses in blazers with inconspicuous Capri pants and plain, flat ballerinas. Although she is considered the wealthiest woman in Germany, she is very restrained about wearing jewelry. Only simple ear clips dangle from her earlobes; her gold wedding ring is on her right ring finger.

Together with her husband and children, the businesswoman lives in a villa surrounded by a wall in Munich's Schwabing district. Only a few people know the family's address. Otherwise, they would probably have to fish mountains of beggars' letters out of their mailbox every day. But the Wagners do not live in dissolute luxury. Even the furnishings of their house are said to be almost unspectacular - one looks in vain for expensive paintings and golden faucets.

But a fortune worth billions is also a burden. Marie often has the feeling that those around her do not perceive her as a person but only measure her by her wealth. "Money doesn't evaluate what or who I am. It draws a curtain in front of me that doesn't show me at all," she complains at one point.

In the summer of 2007, the dutiful 45-year-old decides to take a few days off to unwind. Sleeping, reading, massages, and a whole lot of relaxation are now on her otherwise fully loaded to-do list. The "Lanserhof" in the Austrian Lans seems perfect for it. The spa clinic advertises itself as being "a place of peace and tranquility." The facility counts some celebrities among its guests. When Marie arrives weary in Tyrol, she has no idea that the days in Lans will change her life forever.

At the same time as the billionaire, a tall, lanky man checks into the Lanserhof. He has short brown hair and friendly, gray-blue eyes peer from behind glasses in a delicate frame. When the 41-year-old Swiss man lets his smile play, sympathetic-looking dimples form on his cheeks.

The pretty woman with blond, short hair and a shy smile immediately catches the eye of the talented man, who is fluent in six languages. He nods to her in a friendly manner; tries to attract her attention with success. The attractive Swiss introduces himself to Marie as Helg Sgarbi; by profession, he is a negotiator for the Swiss government in political crisis areas. Over the next few days, the two have long and profound conversations, while together, they go on extensive hikes through the mountains. Marie comes to trust the clever and humorous Swiss.

And so, what happens is completely beyond the behavior of Germany's wealthiest woman: she falls in love with the foreign man. Sgarbi shows his most charming side and ensnares the woman, who makes a lonely and melancholy impression on him. Marie tries to resist the budding feelings. But one evening, the temptation and desire for the smell of foreign skin are greater than misgivings and a sense of duty. The beginning of a passionate, forbidden affair.

Back in Schwabing, the mother of three tries to suppress her guilty conscience and not let on to her husband. While she goes about her business and family life as usual, her thoughts are constantly circling around Helg. The 1.85-meter-tall man has her firmly under his spell. Unbridled passion makes her forget her worries about the impending consequences if the affair is exposed.

But Marie notices that something is bothering her lover. She senses that something is on his mind. Then Helg tells her about his problem. During one of his trips to America, he caused a terrible traffic accident. An innocent child was killed. And as if that wasn't bad enough, the victim's family, who are members of the Italian Mafia, are now threatening him. "What do they want from you?" asked Marie, visibly shocked by the story. "Money. They want 10 million," Helg sighs. "Do you want me to help you?" the 45-year-old offers her affair. At first, the Swiss man rejects his lover's offer - he wants to settle the matter on his own. But Marie senses that Helg is not up to the task. Neither mentally nor financially.

In November 2007, Marie decides to help the 41-year-old out of his predicament. The secret lovers meet in the underground parking garage of a hotel. There, the businesswoman hands Helg 8 million USD in cash - he can siphon off the remaining requested millions from his own assets, he had told her. Visibly relieved by the quick solution to his problem, the man promises her to pay back the money as soon as possible. With interest, of course. Marie is determined: When Helg has paid back the 8 million USD, she wants to donate the sum to a charitable organization. But that's up in the air. All that matters now is that Helg is no longer in danger. After all, the Mafia is not to be trifled with.

Several months have now passed since the family's mother got involved in the passionate affair, and she becomes more and more aware of what is at stake for her. Helg is unattached - but she is not. You don't just throw 17 years of marriage overboard. When the charming Swiss man demands that the businesswoman separate from her husband and join him, she is still torn. But when the 42-year-old suddenly demands 350 million USD to cover his living expenses, the successful businesswoman realizes that he is not concerned with her as a person but with her fortune. Marie would now prefer to simply forget the affair with Helg and continue with her husband Klaus, where she had broken out of the relationship with him. She informs Sgarbi of her decision and does not want to see him again.

A few days later, a courier rings the front doorbell of the Wagner villa in Schwabing. The man hands Marie a brown DIN A4 envelope. The sender has written "Personal" on the letter. The 46-year-old feels sick to her stomach. She hastily tears open the envelope and pulls out a white sheet of paper and some photos. When her eyes fall on the pictures, her body breaks out in a cold sweat. The printouts show her making love to Helg. Panic-stricken, she skims the enclosed letter, which after the first sentence, turns out to be a blackmail letter from none other than Sgarbi himself. He had secretly filmed the forbidden meetings and what happened behind closed doors. In order to prevent the recordings from reaching her husband, her relatives, board members of important companies, and, last but not least, the press, she is supposed to pay him 60 million USD.

Marie's breath quickens more and more as she reads the lines. Her chest rises and falls every second. She ruffles her short hair in despair. "What am I going to do now?" she keeps asking herself. Like a restless tiger in a cage, the businesswoman paces up and down in her living room. Her thoughts circle at breakneck speed. As if suddenly struck by lightning, she stops abruptly. "Who do you think you are, Helg?" she says loudly into the room. The words penetrate her mind like a declaration of war. Determined, Marie takes a breath. Under no circumstances does she want to let it get her down. Attack is the best defense, as we all know. She will take the wind out of the blackmailer's sails. The woman has made a decision.

In the evening, Klaus comes home from a long day at work. The man only needs to take one look at his wife's face to realize that something is wrong. Wordlessly, she holds out the brown envelope to him, along with the salacious photos and the blackmail letter.

For Klaus, what he sees and reads there is initially a shock. Not only has Marie cheated on him with another man, but the rival is also a criminal who wants to destroy the family's good reputation if he doesn't get the incredible sum of 60 million USD from the Wagners.

Despite their crisis, the couple decides to stand up to Helg Sgarbi. Klaus promises Marie that they will get through this together and that he will have her back. The man keeps his promise.

But before the Wagners can come up with a plan for what to do next, the next blackmail letter arrives at the family's Schwabing home - complete with shameful video footage of

Marie and Helg making love. Sgarbi writes that he is reducing his demand to 20 million USD and giving his former lover an ultimatum until January 15, 2008. Otherwise, the video material will be made public.

Marie summons all her courage, overcomes her shame, and sets off for police headquarters. There she tells the officers her story and files a complaint against the unscrupulous blackmailer. The newly awakened fighting spirit in Marie displaces the fear of an impending scandal.

It is January 14, 2008, as Marie, with a dark silk scarf wrapped around her head and her eyes hidden under large sunglasses, makes her way in her BMW to a dreary rest stop in the Austrian community of Vomp in the Tyrolean district of Schwaz. She has arranged a meeting with the blackmailer for today to hand over the money - one day before the ultimatum expires.

But on that cold winter day, not only Helg Sgarbi is arrested. After the failed money delivery, the special "Cobra" unit also handcuffs 61-year-old Ernano Barretta. The Italian had watched the scene in the parking lot and waited for Sgarbi with his loot. Investigators are certain that the short elderly man with a half-bald head is involved in the extortion attempt. In Barretta's brand-new Audi Q7, the police officers discover a small note. In addition to Marie's name, there are three other women's names. While Sgarbi ends up in custody in Munich, the investigators let Barretta go for the time being. But Italian investigators keep an eye on the man, bugging his villa and his car in the hope that they can get their hands on the millions Marie once gave the man in order to allegedly buy her way out of the Italian Mafia.

Only now does the billionaire learn, bit by bit, who the man really is, who first wrapped her around his finger and then tried to threaten and blackmail her.

Helg Russak, as he was then known, was born in 1965 into a well-off family in the Swiss city of Winterthur, northeast of Zurich. His father was the director of a mechanical engineering company with over a thousand employees. Helg has another younger sister, who moves abroad as an adult. The parents teach their children early on how to appear self-confident and teach them mannerly behavior. Due to the Russaks' love of travel, the siblings learn about the diversity of other cultures at an early age. As a young man, Helg decides to study law at a university in Zurich. After finishing his studies, the Swiss worked for a credit institute until he was 31 when a high-tech company offered him a lucrative job. But then, the first break in the man's biography occurs. From 1999 to 2001, Russak allegedly stayed in Europe as well as in North and South America and earned his living as a "gambler," as the Bülach District Court later paraphrased it.

At the end of the nineties or the beginning of the two-thousands, Russak met Ernano Barretta, who was in his mid-fifties.

The Italian, whom outsiders call a charismatic manipulator, describes himself as a "miracle healer and messenger of God." At the beginning of the 1990s, the self-proclaimed guru, who came to Switzerland as a guest worker when he was young, gathered a few followers around him - mostly young lawyers from Zurich.

Barretta can walk on water and heal sick people with the power of God; as with Jesus on the cross, fresh blood then flows abruptly from his hands, feet, and chest, his followers recount. The guru makes his disciples give him a large part of their monthly wages. Barretta's female followers are rewarded by having sex with the guru. The Italian claims that his semen is the blood of Jesus Christ. His ejaculation of semen during a physical union, the man believes, heals the receiving woman.

Around the mid-nineties, his followers follow him to the Italian region of Abruzzo to Pescosansonesco. The cult leader has his male disciples toil on a construction site while the women do all the work at hand in an exquisite country hotel he has built. In the Italian investigation files, one can later read: "The followers were psychologically influenced and used like slaves for work." But the guru doesn't just let his followers work themselves to death physically; Barretta also harnesses them to criminal schemes, such as fake fundraisers.

Only for Helg Russak does Barretta envisage a different task. Even the cult leader is not unaware of the attractiveness and charisma of the now 35-year-old Swiss, who has completely fallen for believing in the Italian guru. From then on, Russak tours luxurious hotels and trendy bars all over Europe - always on the lookout for his next potential victim. Helg is on the lookout for wealthy ladies who make a lonely impression on him. He then turns on the charm and makes the chosen one feel like a desirable and interesting woman - regardless of her possessions.

One of his first victims, with whose feelings he plays, is the now deceased 83-year-old Comtesse Alissa*. After Russak becomes aware of the Swiss Comtesse, he travels to Monte-Carlo to gain her trust. His charm soon shows success. He sends roses to the Comtesse in her suite and quickly wraps the older woman around his finger. He offers her his help if needed - after all, he is a lawyer and banker. The 36-year-old also makes a strong impression on acquaintances of the Comtesse.

Only a short time after the meeting, Helg and Alissa talk about getting married. Despite her 83 years, the widow believes she has found love once again in her life. She trusts Russak without hesitation - this is the only way to explain the fact that the elderly lady signs over most of her fortune to the Swiss.

Some of the countess'scountess's friends, however, suspect a plot. They discover that there seems to be a large number of well-heeled women who have fallen for Russak's charms and feel exploited by him. In one fell swoop, the confidants bring the Comtesse back down to earth. There is no longer any talk of marriage - the 83-year-old wants her money back. Only when Russak gives her back part of her fortune does she stop her court action against the gigolo.

In 2003, Helg Russak marries Gabriele, four years younger, also a follower of the guru Ernano Barretta. The Swiss takes her last name and, from then on, is called Sgarbi.

In the same year, the woman whisperer is tried for the first time in Bülach, Switzerland, and receives a six-month prison sentence - suspended. Karla*, a confidante of the Comtesse, had followed in the footsteps of her friend's new partner. She also stalked Barretta. Soon, she was blatantly telling Sgarbi's entourage that the Swiss man was a cheating gigolo and that his crony Ernano should be treated with extreme caution.

However Sgarbi went about it, the initially suspicious Karla ended up in his bed. Later work colleagues of Helg, on the other hand, can very well explain how it could come to all the events. "Helg made everyone feel special," one co-worker later recalled, "he scanned you in seconds and recognized your weak points. And then explained, I know how to help you." Shortly before Sgarbi leaves that very workplace, he asks one of his colleagues to join him. In an ominous voice, the Swiss says goodbye to the young man with the words, "One day you will hear things from me for which you will hate and curse me. Like everyone else, you will judge me." Another companion recalls, "Helg told countless stories about himself, and in the end, you didn't know anything about him. Not a thing."

At the last meeting between Helg and Karla in February 2002, she had no idea that a video camera was rolling during the lovemaking session. Only a few days after the lustful meeting, Karla held an envelope in her hands. Inside was the videotape with sexually explicit content and a threatening letter. She was not to interfere in other people's affairs. Karla, however, did not let herself be blackmailed - the woman filed a complaint against her former lover.

However, a suspended sentence could not deter him. In December 2005, Sgarbi lays in wait again, this time at the Swiss Grand Hotel Quellenhof. Soon he has his next victim in sight. Helga* has taken a fancy to the gigolo - the wife of a rich furniture manufacturer. He sweet-talks the married woman. The two begin an affair. Only a short time later, he tells the unsuspecting woman the story that he will later tell again and again in slimmed-down versions: he had a terrible traffic accident in America. He tells Helga that a child was seriously injured in the accident and that he now has to pay an enormous sum in damages to the parents. Otherwise, he would face a prison sentence. 1.6 million USD would be demanded. So, he manages to wrest 750000 USD from his well-heeled mistress - the other missing half he could raise himself.

But Sgarbi can't get enough. At the end of January 2007, the Swiss confesses to his mistress that he secretly recorded their sex act together and saved the files on his laptop. Unfortunately, however, his computer was stolen during a trip to Italy. And now the Italian Mafia is blackmailing him and demanding 1.8 million USD - otherwise, both their lives are in danger. Helga believes Sgarbi. Driven by fear, she hands him the demanded sum a few days later.

At that point, the woman still has the hope that her lover will regard the money as a loan and pay it back to her as soon as possible. When she asks, Sgarbi can't help laughing. "You'll never see that money again," he replies with a sneer. But the Swiss man shows no sign of shame or remorse. On the contrary, he demands that Helga rent him an apartment in Barcelona, Spain.

The woman denies him his wish but can't let go of him; that's how much she has fallen for his charm. Not even a year later, in November 2007, he begins to blackmail Helga. Now he tells her that he himself is in possession of the shameful film footage. Sgarbi wants 2.5 million USD from his affair. Otherwise, he will send the material to her family, friends, and acquaintances. Helga doesn't know what to do. She calls in a lawyer to assist her. But before Sgarbi gets around to taking the million-dollar sum from the woman, he is arrested by the police.

In the summer of 2007, while still having an affair with Helga and trying to cheat her out of her money, Sgarbi checks in twice at the Lanserhof - his new, lucrative hunting ground. First, he stalks the businesswoman Marianne*. The successful lady succumbs to the charm of the woman whisperer - but she won't give him any money. The situation is different with the wealthy Bavarian entrepreneur Sarah*. With one of his invented stories, he convinces the woman to give him $350,000 - then contact breaks off. Sarah is just one of four women whom the gigolo defrauds of considerable sums using the same scam over and over again.

But neither Sarah nor any of the other women are of the caliber of his next victim. With the business card Marie gives him, Sgarbi sits down at his laptop and researches the woman on the Internet. Bull's eye!

Barretta, who presumably profits to a large extent from Sgarbi's scammed money, secretly films Helg and Marie's passionate union from the next room. At first, Sgarbi tells the billionaire the fairy tale of the Mafia child he killed in a car accident, and in this way, he gets his first million. When Marie ends the affair, however, Sgarbi shows his true colors and sends her the first blackmail letter with the shameful photos.

In May 2009, Helg Sgarbi goes on trial at the Munich I Regional Court. The defendant makes a comprehensive confession through his lawyer. This spares the victimized women from having to testify in court. It is a lightning trial. On the same day, the presiding judge sentences Sgarbi to six years imprisonment for commercial fraud and attempted commercial extortion. The public prosecutor initially agrees with the sentence; however, he is disappointed with the course of the proceedings. Although the accused has made a comprehensive confession, Sgarbi leaves it open where the investigators can find the scammed millions and the sex tapes. Nor does the defendant reveal what role the guru Ernano Barretta plays in the crimes. Nevertheless, Marie is satisfied with the verdict against her adversary.

In the summer of 2012, the authorities also put Barretta before an Italian court. Marie appears as a joint plaintiff. The judge acquits the self-proclaimed guru of the charge of forming a criminal organization. However, the 65-year-old is sentenced to seven and a half years in prison for serious fraud. Barretta appeals; however, the sentence becomes final in 2014. The judge acquits all other six defendants, including Barretta's wife and two of his adult children, of all charges.

Marie continues to fight. In December 2013, her then-lover was supposed to be a free man again. But after his release from Landsberg prison, the Swiss man only makes it as far as the border of his home country. At the border in Lörrach, police officers arrest him again. Marie had wanted a statement of assets from Sgarbi via a bailiff, but he refused. She wants to know where her millions are. In addition, she has bought two other aggrieved women, their titles obtained in court against the gigolo. The businesswoman is now demanding a total of 11 million USD from the blackmailer. Marie, therefore, applies to the Landsberg district court for compulsory detention against her former lover. In the summer of 2014, Sgarbi is finally released. Marie's claim to her money, however, is subject to a 30-year statute of limitations.

Whether she will ever see her money again remains an open question. Giving up is not an option for Marie. She wants to continue to fight the gigolo and his machinations - for herself and for all the other victims. But the story has left scars on the woman's soul. After what happened, the billionaire lives even more withdrawn and is even more suspicious than before. In 2018, Marie and her husband Klaus announce their separation - amicably.

It has become quiet around Ernano Barretta. After his imprisonment, nothing more has become publicly known about him. The release of the 74-year-old must have taken place, purely mathematically, in 2022.

Whether the marriage to Sgarbi's wife still continues today is also not publicly known. Nor whether the Swiss is still a supporter of Barretta. The fact is, however, that the convicted fraudster will make headlines again in 2020. Since 2017, Sgarbi has been in a relationship with former well-heeled Chanel model Alexandra Haack. The lady dies of natural causes in March 2020 at the age of 79.

The sole heir to her fortune is her partner, Helg Sgarbi.

»It is better to fail with honor than to succeed by cheating.

- Sophokles (497 v. Chr.–405 v. Chr.),
Greek Fleet commander and politician –

CHAPTER 5

ONE MILLION SORROWS

Diana can't remember the last time she was this tense. Her hands were wet with sweat. Her entire body is frozen to stone. Add to that the unbearable heat of the headlights.

"Give me the check," she hears the man's voice, which seems far away. He is wearing a black suit, along with a light gray shirt and an anthracite tie. His wrinkled face has a serious expression, and his blond hair is neatly parted to the right.

Sitting across from him is her husband, Charles. He is wearing a light blue polo shirt with a dark gray collar and colored sleeves. He has his eyes closed; his heart beats firmly against his chest. He senses that in a few moments, both of their lives will change forever - no matter how this turns out.

Close to a nervous breakdown, his wife Diana also closes her eyes and leans against the soft seat cushion of the bench. What if it does go wrong? All this time, Charles had been lucky, but round after round, he was getting closer and closer to defeat.

Then the moderator finally announces the correct answer to the all-important million-dollar question.

Four years earlier - Celador's offices

"The concept must be easy to understand - questions and answers."

"Oh, come on, Paul. People want to see something spectacular. We're not in our fifties anymore."

On a rainy day in October 1997, CEO Paul Smith and his three employees, Steven Knight, David Briggs, and Mike Whitehill, are in the conference room of Celador, a British production company. The aim of their meeting is to gather ideas for a new game show format for the broadcaster ITV (Independent Television).

However, this turns out to be more difficult than expected because the television market has changed a lot over the past few years. Gone are the days when classic, light entertainment provided high ratings. People want something new; they want to stare spellbound at the screen and feel emotions.

Celador believes it has found the solution with a show under the working title 'CASH MOUNTAIN.' The concept of the show is a simple one, but in the eyes of the creators, it is all the more ingenious: the candidate is asked a question that is endowed with a certain amount of money. The player has four possible answers to choose from, only one of which is the correct one. Three "helping hands" are available to him as support, but he may only use them once in the course of the game. For example, the candidate can call a friend, have two answers eliminated to make the question a 50/50 chance, and ask the audience. Round after round, the level of difficulty increases, and with it, the prize sum for each question - until the last question is about a million pounds. If a question is answered incorrectly, the candidate is knocked back to the next security level. In this case, these are 1,000 and 32,000 pounds, respectively. If the contestant has reached the marks, at least he won't go home empty-handed if he answers incorrectly.

When he hears this rough draft for the first time, ITV program director David Liddiment is not particularly taken with it at first. He still doesn't quite understand where the thrill is supposed to be in this.

"The audience is up close and personal with life-changing decisions," explain Celador boss Paul Smith and David Briggs. They say the contestants can be seen going through the full range of emotions. Since Liddiment is still not completely convinced, the two let him play a game of 'CASH MOUNTAIN' himself, during which the program director slowly recognizes the potential of the show and asks Celador to produce a pilot, i.e., a test program.

After Chris Tarrant, born in 1946 in Reading, Berkshire, had agreed to host the show, the applications of interested participants were received by phone, and the concept was tweaked a bit. The recording of the first episode soon took place. The studio is set up like an arena and can accommodate several hundred viewers. The ten contestants are all seated in a semicircle around the "center" of the studio, where the actual game takes place. There, the moderator's seat and the candidate's seat and screens face each other.

In order to reach the middle and thus have a chance of winning one million pounds, the candidates first compete against each other in a selection round. They have to put the answers to a question in the right order within 20 seconds. A computer then determines the fastest candidate from the correct answers. The fastest candidate can then take a seat in the middle and play for large sums of money.

Despite a rather bumpy start, the new quiz show has also been well-received by TV viewers. The correspondingly high ratings prompt Liddiment to show the program in a daily format on prime-time television. However, he sets one condition: a new name for the show is to be found.

Inspired by this great news, Smith and his staff are now full of beans, tweaking the look of the format. Among other things, speakers will be built into the contestants' chairs to make the vibrations of the sound perceptible and the adrenaline even greater. Furthermore, the lighting mood in the studio is supposed to express the candidate's inner pressure: the higher he climbs up the question tree, the darker it is supposed to get in the room. In this way, the already tense contestant feels completely on his own when it comes to the higher prize sums, which creates additional nervousness. In the same breath, Keith Strachan and his son Matthew compose suitable pieces of music. These are characterized mainly by their exciting bass beats and tense woodwinds, which, for the sake of dramaturgy, are played an octave higher round after round. It is also the music that ultimately inspires the creators to give the show its new name: 'Who Wants to Be a Millionaire?' - true to the song of the same name by Cole Porter.

The program celebrated its premiere on September 04, 1998. From then on, one in three British households is glued to the screen every week to watch the thrill of winning a million pounds. In its heyday, ITV reached an average of around 19 million viewers with the show. The concept is so successful that TV stations from America and other parts of Europe are soon interested.

"*On 'Who Wants to Be a Millionaire,*' all you have to do is answer 15 multiple-choice questions to win a million pounds! Apply now at the following number and enter! It couldn't be easier!"

Even as Tarrant's voice echoes through the living room, Adrian Pollock is already reaching for the phone and dialing the number shown on the screen. The IT consultant from the Vale of Glamorgan in Wales is a self-confessed quiz fan and, together with his father and sister Diana, regularly takes part in quiz nights in bars and pubs. For this reason, the entire family gets together on the couch on *Who Wants to Be a Millionaire'* nights and feverishly guesses along. Adrian, in particular, takes a liking to the show and, over the next few years, develops a real obsession. His enthusiasm goes so far that the fanatic tries to apply dozens of times. However, the rush is so high that Adrian is not put through even after several attempts.

It sounds so simple: call the station, get a positive response, and then wait for the editorial staff to call back, where you are asked a guessing question. The person whose answer is closest to the correct solution gets the chance to take part in the show. This system is psychologically designed to keep people calling back over and over again.

In the end, it took Adrian almost 1700 calls to finally make it to the longed-for 'hot seat' in the middle of the studio on December 23, 2000; before that, he had already been on the show three times as a selected candidate. The rules state that a contestant can apply and participate in the show as many times as they want - as long as they don't make it to Chris Tarrant in the middle. Once you've been there and had your chance at a million pounds, you're never allowed to compete again after that. The only exception is for celebrity specials.

Adrian's dream of winning the grand prize ended after question 10 - the 32,000-pound question. Until then, he still had all three jokers at his disposal. But in question 11, he was so lost that he not only used up all his jokers but also gave the wrong answer. So, he has to leave the show with 32,000 pounds.

Since the IT guy still cannot be dissuaded from his obsession and hopes for the big money, he persuades his sister Diana to apply as a candidate as well. Although she is luckier and makes it not only into the show but onto the chair on her first attempt, she also fails the 64,000-pound question and goes home with 32,000 pounds.

There, her defeat still resonates weeks later. She mopes and racks her brains, day in and day out, over her early elimination. The whole affair gets to the point that it results in more and more frequent discussions with her husband, Charles. He accuses her of only thinking about this "stupid game show" and that nothing else can bring her happiness. Diana then replies, hurt, that this is not fair and that their joint family always supported Charles in everything he did. Now it would be up to him to support his family.

September 09, 2001 - Elstree Film & Television Studios, Borehamwood, England

In the canteen room of the studio 'Who Wants to Be a Millionaire,' there is a boisterous atmosphere. The ten contestants for the upcoming show sit together and make small talk as they eat lunch together. Despite the friendly atmosphere, a certain restraint resonates - after all, they would soon become rivals in the dreaded selection round. Among them is Charles Ingram, who traveled with his wife Diana from Easterton, a village in the county of Wiltshire. The 38-year-old is a medium-sized man with broad shoulders, light hair, and thin lips. His wife is half a head shorter than him, has long black hair, and wears a magenta top under a dark blazer with patterns.

To some, Diana's friendly face may look familiar. A few months earlier, the kindergarten teacher had also participated in the show and even made it to Chris Tarrant's chair. The game ended for her after the £32,000 question.

After the meal, the candidates are asked one by one for a preliminary interview so that they can tell interesting facts and stories about their lives. Afterward, at 3:00 p.m. sharp, they go straight to the studio. There, not only are the participants' wardrobes checked for camera suitability, but the broadcast sequence is also rehearsed in detail.

It is a strange feeling for all of them to enter the set they are so familiar with from television. And so, the candidates are surprised not only by its surprising compactness but also by how "shabby" the set looks when viewed up close. Almost all the props have wood on the back; there are small scratches and marks everywhere. In television, a lot of things are more appearance than reality.

After the rehearsal, dinner is served in the canteen before the millionaire candidates wait in their dressing rooms for the broadcast to begin. They use this time for final mental preparation, to freshen up, and to inform their chosen telephone jokers of a few rules.

At just before 7:00 p.m., Charles and Diana are picked up by a member of the production team and brought down to the studio. While the escorts take their seats in the audience, the candidates get the final touches in makeup; then, one by one, they are called up by warm-up man Ray Turner and welcomed into the studio to thunderous applause from the audience already there. Again, it's a strange feeling - like being the last to show up at a party that's already in full swing.

The ten candidates settle down at their assigned computers. There are a few seconds of tense silence until suddenly, the familiar theme tune is heard, the audience applauds, and the presenter steps in front of the cameras. The broadcast has begun; everything is going like clockwork. No one suspects that this recording will go down in the history of *'Who Wants to Be a Millionaire.'*

No sooner has Tarrant greeted the audience than nervousness sets in among all the candidates in the studio. Now it's getting serious. Who will make it to the middle?

"Put this title of an Agatha Christie novel in the right order:

  A: Nile
  B: On
  C: Death
  D   The"

The candidates now have twenty seconds to complete the task. As their fingers frantically scurry across the keys, some look resigned, and others catch a glimpse of their seatmate's monitor.

"Actually, not that hard," says the moderator, eyeing the tense faces of the participants, "but let's see who has figured out the solution. *Death on the Nile*."

A graphic displays the names of the candidates; behind them, the number of seconds.

"And the fastest was … Charles Ingram with 3.97 seconds!"

Charles puts his head back in relief, takes a deep breath, and stands up. After he has settled into the coveted chair, Tarrant and he chats a bit more about the candidate's life so far.

Charles William Ingram was born on August 6, 1963, in Shardlow, a village in the central English county of Derbyshire, the son of retired RAF (Royal Air Force) squadron commander John Ingram and his wife, set designer Susan. The boy attended the prestigious Oswestry School and was commissioned as a probationary officer in the Royal Engineers in 1986. After being promoted to Captain and then Major in each of 1990 and 1995, he served first in Northern Ireland and then on the NATO peacekeeping mission in Bosnia for six months in February 2000. In August of that year, he graduated from Cranfield University with a master's degree in business management.

After the little chat, the moderator welcomes Charles' companion - his wife Diana - to the audience and then explains the rules of the game again.

"Fifteen questions, three jokers - if he answers all 15 right, he wins a million pounds. We're starting a new round of *Who Wants to Be a Millionaire!*" Tarrant lets the tension rise.

On cue, all the spotlights in the studio turn to "the middle," accompanied by the sound of drums.

The first five questions pose no problem whatsoever for the major. In no time at all, Charles reaches the first security level at 1,000 pounds, although the initial nervousness still doesn't seem to have completely dissipated. Again and again, he tugs at his neck, runs his hand through his light hair, and, laughing insecurely, claims to have "definitely" given the wrong answer.

For the first third of the game, Charles' worries are largely unfounded. But no sooner has the second period began with the £2,000 question than the first joker has to take the fall.

"I know that!" Tarrant introduces the question, looking at his monitor. "*Who in 'Coronation Street'* ... I bet you don't know the answer!" he adds with a laugh, "When was the last time you watched the show 'Coronation Street'?"

"Never," Charles counters. "I mean, I`ve seen it a few times while zipping through, but never followed it."

"Just look at the question ..." the moderator reassures him. "... And decide how you want to proceed.

In 'Coronation Street,' who is Audrey's daughter?

   A: Janice
   B: Gail
   C: Linda
   D: Sally"

"I really have absolutely no idea," Charles says, shaking his head.

"You still have all three wild cards," Tarrant reminds him. "You can poll the audience, call a friend, or have the computer erase two wrong answers."

Charles nods and opts for the audience wild card, whereupon the moderator reads the question again, this time directed to the audience. They now have the opportunity to choose the correct answer using a remote control at their seat. There are four buttons on the keypad with the letters A, B, C, and D. A computer then calculates the answers. A computer then converts the votes cast into percentages and displays them on a graph.

In Charles' case, the system calculates four percent each for answers A and D, 89 percent for answer B, and three percent for answer C.

"It's not easy to decide," Tarrant jokes. "But it's entirely up to you."

"You're right about that," Charles counters with a grin. "But if I'm wrong, at least I can claim at home and at work that it's not my fault. So, I'll trust the public and vote 'Gail'."

The answer is logged, and the presenter announces that the major is now £2,000 richer. While the applause of the audience prevails for a few seconds, Charles also joins in it as a sign of thanks to the audience.

After this small intermediate hurdle, the candidate turns all his focus to the subsequent 4,000-pound question. Tarrant wants to know in which part of the United Kingdom the River Foyle can be found. Contrary to his hopes, however, this question does not play into Charles' cards either. He decides to go for the support of his friend Gerald. Hastily, as there are only 30 seconds, the major reads the question to his telephone joker along with the four possible answers.

"Northern Ireland," it resounds from the studio speakers as if shot out of a pistol.

"How sure are you?" Charles wants to know after a relieved sigh.

"It's not exactly emotionally easy being on the other end of the line from Who Wants to Be a Millionaire," Gerald jokes. "But I'm 99 percent sure."

"All right, that's fine," Charles replies. "Thank you."

Shortly thereafter, time runs out, and the phone call ends.

"He sounded very sure," Tarrant summarizes. "Would you like to try?"

"Yes," Charles says. "Since he has the memory of an encyclopedia, I'll trust him and go with 'Northern Ireland.'"

The answer is logged, and after a small pause for suspense, Tarrant resolves:

"The answer is correct! 4,000 pounds are yours."

Again, the audience applauds; Charles puffs out a sigh of relief. He is made to realize with all his might that the road to the longed-for million is anything but easy. Tarrant, too, senses that his candidate needs a motivational boost and leans forward.

"Well played," he declares as he shakes Charles' hand.

No sooner has the applause died down than a long-drawn horn blares through the studio - the show is over.

"Oh no," Charles groans, slapping his hand over his face with a shy laugh. He seems embarrassed by his performance in front of the audience of millions. "That means I have to come back tomorrow," he concludes.

"Yes, that's the 'good' news, Charles," Tarrant jibes with a laugh. "You will return to us tomorrow! And also joining us are the following ten candidates."

As the presenter announces the names of the contestants eager to win the next show, Charles' wife's ears perk up at one of them in particular: Tecwen Whittock, 50, a lecturer in business administration at the university in Pontypridd - a town of 33,000 in southern Wales.

As luck would have it, the major's wife is in possession of the university professor's telephone number. She got it from her brother Adrian, who trained his dexterity in the course of preparing for the show by means of a specially created fastest-finger machine, causing a stir among some applicants - including the aforementioned university professor. He gave Adrian his number because he was interested in such a device.

Thinking that her husband could use a little help on his way to making a million, Diana types Whittock's number into her phone that very evening.

Because of his scatterbrainedness, no one involved in the show believes the major will make it too far. For one thing, his self-doubt is too great, and for another, he has already wasted two of the three jokers after the first seven questions. Although it's not impossible for him to make it to the million mark completely on his own, this is a highly demanding task even for experienced quiz experts. For a candidate like Charles, on the other hand, the early loss of all jokers is usually a quick death sentence. With a lot of luck, however, the major may be able to double his previous winnings.

Question three - second, third

"... there are still eight questions separating him from the million - for which he has only the fifty-fifty joker left. Let's start with *Who Wants to Be a Millionaire!*"

Now it's getting serious. The spotlights in the studio focus on the candidate and presenter, accompanied by the already familiar sound of drums.

"At this point, we should adjust the strategy a little bit," Tarrant wants to lighten the mood, not suspecting that after this recording, Charles will actually secure a place in the show's history for that very reason. "You have already earned a profit of 4,000 pounds, with which you can exit at any time. But of course, I also know that the higher prize money is tempting. Let's look at the 8,000 pounds question first. And here it comes:

Who was Jacqueline Kennedy's second husband?

A: Adnan Khashoggi
B: Ronald Reagan
C: Aristotle Onassis
D: Rupert Murdoch"

Charles seems to have used the pause between notes to tweak his approach to solving the questions. For example, if before he immediately complained about having no idea and answering incorrectly, he now takes his time and goes through the question again step by step.

"All right ... I'm not sure ... but I think it's Aristotle Onassis ..."

A cough from the audience breaks the tension. Neither Charles nor Tarrant are fazed by it, however.

"What for?" the moderator asks.

"Well, so I mean ... Ronald Reagan ... I know who he is, and I don't remember him ever being married to Jacqueline Kennedy. But Aristotle Onassis rings a bell ..."

Charles asks to be allowed to run through the answer choices again in his head but continues to lean toward answer C.

"I'll go with Aristotle Onassis," he finally says firmly.

"You are a wild and crazy man!" realizes Tarrant. "Is that your final word?"

"You only live once," counters the major with a laugh. "Yes, I'll take it."

Answer C is highlighted in yellow. The sign that the candidate has made his final choice.

"Are you happy with your new strategy?" the moderator tries to drag out the resolution a bit.

"No," Charles replies. "But it's too late now."

As they both laugh, Tarrant declares the answer correct.

"It still seems to add up, though," he counters, as the audience's applause dies down.

Take your time, play the question over and over in your head, and guess your way to the correct answer in the end. This method also works well for the £16,000 question. Will Charles be able to crack the million mark? But before that can happen, the major must first face the 32,000-pound question - and sees his promising start shatter into a thousand pieces.

"Who published a British hit album in 2000 called 'Born to Do It'?

    A: Coldplay
    B: Toploader
    C: A1
    D: Craig David"

For quite a while, Charles remains silent with a thoughtful expression, visibly panting in exasperation - another one of those questions.

"Craig David ... honestly, I don't think I've ever heard of him ..." he says as the director shows his wife rolling her eyes. " ... There's no point. I have to take the fifty-fifty joker."

"Of course - that's what the jokers are for," Tarrant blithely counters. "Computer, cross out two wrong answers, please."

Immediately, 'Coldplay' and 'Toploader' disappear, whereupon Charles now leans toward answer C. As the candidate is about to log his choice, something strange happens. Diana Ingram seems to have suddenly developed dry throat problems because she coughs three times in a row, followed by quiet throat clearing. Although she tries to be as discreet as possible and holds her hand over her mouth, the microphone on her lapel records the sounds clearly and audibly. Immediately after her cough has subsided, Charles suddenly wants to log in Answer D after all. Is it just a coincidence?

"You know, I'm wrong 80 percent of the time when I guess," Charles reasons. "So, I go with 'Craig David.'"

Tarrant can't help but laugh in disbelief and covers his eyes with one hand.

"Last word?"

"I'm guessing 'Craig David,' " the candidate confirms.

The answer is then logged. A short commercial break follows, then the moderator verifies the guess as correct. Now Charles has not only reached the second security level but also has the same winning amount as Diana and his brother-in-law safely in his pocket. Can the major equal this and perhaps even pocket more money? What at the beginning looked like a quickly sealed end to the game gradually develops into a promising battle for a million pounds.

Alongside all the admiration and disbelief, however, there are also initial doubts because, meanwhile, the major's strange about-turn is also causing a stir behind the scenes. The team around managing director Adrian Woolfe suspects that something is not right. How else could it be explained that Charles claims to have no clue round after round, only to end up guessing the right answer?

Statistically, the probability of giving the right answer to a question is 25 percent. This means that randomly choosing the right answer is just as likely as randomly choosing the wrong answer. It might work a few times - but can a person really be so lucky as to succeed with it on just about every question?

Not wanting to jump to conclusions and lacking solid evidence, the staff limit themselves for now to keeping an eye on Charles via the control room monitors. Neither he nor anyone else at the studio suspects anything about the slowly burgeoning allegations of fraud.

"I haven't the faintest idea how you come up with a man you've never heard of before!" Tarrant lets out, dumbfounded, handing the contestant a handwritten check. "Anyway - you're up to £32,000. Next up is question 11, for which you're out of jokers. However, should you answer incorrectly, you would still be left with the 32,000 pounds in any case. All right! Let's take a look at question number 11, which is worth 64,000 pounds:

'Gentleman v Players' was an annual event between Amateurs and professionals of which sport?

    A: Lawn tennis
    B: Fifteen-a-side rugby
    C: Polo
    D: Cricket"

As one is already used to from him, Charles looks at his screen for a long time. As he does so, he places the index finger of his right hand over his mouth.

"It could actually be any of these," he says. "But I think it's cricket."

As Charles explains that he thinks he remembers a corresponding image from that event, a cough is heard from the direction of the candidates.

"Take your time," Tarrant advises him, but Charles does not respond. He's once again busy reciting the answer choices.

"It could be lawn tennis ..." he thinks aloud. "Or maybe polo? I'm doing it again, sorry," he adds with an embarrassed laugh and then continues to think for quite a while. "I don't think it's fifteen-a-side rugby. And I'm not guessing lawn tennis or polo, either. If I had to guess - and I definitely can - I'd go with cricket."

Another cough.

"Yeah, I'll take it. Last word."

Charles' choice is logged.

"You're on £32,000 - the same amount your wife won with us," Tarrant introduces the resolution. "And you've just won £64,000!"

Thunderous applause immediately erupts in the studio. The audience can't believe the scenes they've just been treated to up close.

"For a man who's never heard of Craig David, you're doing amazingly well!"

Charles also does 'amazingly well' on questions 12 and 13, following the familiar pattern of listening to the question, claiming not to know the answer, reading out the answer choices again aloud, tending towards the wrong answer, only to turn the wheel at the last moment and tap on the correct answer. At this point, it's no longer just the production team that suspects the major's game might be rigged. Some of the candidates in the studio are also beginning to have doubts.

"The next question is worth 500,000 pounds. And it is as follows:

Baron Haussmann is known for planning which city?

> A: *Rome*
> B: *Paris*
> C: *Berlin*
> D: *Athens.*"

"I think it's Berlin," Charles answers confidently, whereupon Tarrant grips his forehead, smiling in bewilderment. "I think!" the candidate follows up.

"Charles, ten minutes ago, you thought it was the band 'A1,'" Tarrant retorts.

This sobering realization amuses the major but plausibly justifies his choice by saying that 'Haussmann' sounds very German. As he persists, repeating Berlin over and over to himself, another cough is heard. This time, however, the sound is followed by what sounds like a cross between a throat clearing and 'No' - the English word for 'no.' A nearly 30-second pause for thought ensues, with Charles' tense gasps mingling with the torturous heartbeats of the background music. To this, the candidate leans forward and rests his head on his left arm.

"I just can't figure it out," he mumbles. "I don't think it's Paris ..."

No sooner has the last word left his lips than another cough sounds. Charles seems to be thinking more carefully now.

"I'm ruling out Athens and Rome in any case. While I initially thought it would be Berlin, there is a possibility that Paris may be correct ..."

Another long pause.

"I've read that somewhere before ..." he frets. "I think it's Berlin ... or is it Paris?"

"You don't have to play that question," the moderator intervenes. "You have a check for £250,000 to go home with. On the other hand, you could also make it 500,000 pounds if you give me the right answer."

The candidate is also aware of this and thinks feverishly one last time.

"Yes, I think it's Paris ..."

This is followed by the third cough within this round.

"I'll gamble!" Charles then announces, nodding. Apparently, greed for money prevails.

The presenter, however, does not want to accept this frivolity so easily because of the considerable prize money and repeats what is at stake. Charles, on the other hand, can no longer be dissuaded from his decision and logs in answer B.

"You already owned 250,000 pounds, and you didn't have to play that question," Tarrant says with raised eyebrows. "All this time you thought it was 'Berlin, Berlin, Berlin' and finally changed your mind ... this just earned you 500,000 pounds!"

"YES!" shouts Charles, jumping to his feet. The audience explodes.

The scatterbrained major, who no one thought would even make it past the 8,000-pound question, is now actually facing the million-dollar question. Will he also be able to answer these correctly and be crowned the third main winner of the show?

While the people in the studio unsuspectingly express their enthusiasm behind the scenes, the mood is like that of a funeral.

The employees are displeased that their game seems to have been "hacked" and are feverishly searching for the loophole in the system. Is Charles possibly getting the correct answers via the vibrations of a pager? Since the studio signal is not encrypted, it would be possible to pick up the appropriate frequency on the production floor and listen in on the broadcast. The assistant would then only have to look up the correct answer and dial the number of the device. But does Charles really deserve the title of a criminal mastermind?

Another form of fraud seems more plausible to the team: acoustic signals. This suspicion hardens when a few coughs from the direction of the candidates are localized behind Charles via the ceiling microphones. What is striking here is the regularity and timing of the sounds. Whenever the major plays the options aloud, a cough can be heard in the correspondingly correct answer. Would this also explain his abrupt change of heart?

"Are you all right?" asks Tarrant. Charles has his elbows pressed into his thighs and his face buried in his sweaty hands.

"No!" he replies with a laugh. "Definitely not."

"This proves what you've accomplished. Take it.", The presenter hands Charles a check in the amount of 500,000 pounds. The latter accepts it with the beaming eyes of a little boy. "All right, we're going to do what I'm sure the entire United Kingdom is waiting for: we're going to take a look at the 1-million-pound question - something we don't do very often since we went on-air with this show three years ago.

A one followed by one hundred zeros is known by what name?

    A: *Googol*
    B: *Megatron*
    C: *Gigabit*
    D: *Nanomole*"

"All right, let's take a look," Charles sighs after looking at the screen in silence for a few seconds. "I'm not sure, but ..."

Tarrant covers his eyes, speechless.

"Charles, you haven't been sure since question two!" he says to laughter from the audience.

"The doubts have doubled since then ...," Charles counters.

"No one will blame you if you quit. 500,000 pounds is a considerable sum," says the presenter. At this moment, the studio microphones record a conversation between Tecwen Whittock and another candidate: the university professor wants to know if his opponent knows the answer to the question, to which the latter replies "Yes" and whisperingly tells him the solution. Not 3 meters away in front of them, Charles once again presents his proven strategy to an audience of millions.

"I think it's 'Nanomole'. Whereas it could also be 'gigabit' ..." he ponders. "I'm not sure I can play that question ... God ... 'Megatron' I'm also ruling out, and I have to confess I can't remember anything like a 'googol' either ..."

A cough.

"Googol ... Googol, Googol," Charles reels off with a thoughtful expression. His voice sounds as if he suddenly does remember something. "By process of elimination, I would say the correct answer is 'googol.' However, I can't tell what that is supposed to be."

"Similarly, you came up with 'Craig David,'" Tarrant replies wryly, "it was him, but you never heard of him."

"I think 'Gigabit', 'Nanomole' and 'Megatron' are wrong ..." continues Charles, "I really think it's 'Googol' ..."

Cough number two within this round sounds through the studio.

"You thought it was 'Nanomole' at first ..." the moderator notes, "you've supposedly never heard of a 'googol'."

Is Tarrant, too, beginning to suspect that something is amiss here?

"I know," Charles counters, "but it's not 'Gigabit' or 'Nanomole' or 'Megatron.' So it must be 'googol' ... which I honestly don't know what that is supposed to be ..."

In the last sentence, the image switches to Diana. She removes her hands pressed to her cheeks from her face and looks first at the ceiling and then to the right with a bewildered expression.

"It's probably the only chance I'll ever have in my life to win a million pounds."

"Charles, it's equally the only chance you have of losing 468,000 pounds," Tarrant sneers. "Let me recap: you have half a million and you want to take the answer you've never heard of? Just for the reason that you've never heard of it? It's entirely up to you and I'm not going to influence you, but again, you could walk out of here with 500,000 pounds."

"I don't mind taking a risk or two," Charles counters, while his wife looks like she's on the verge of a nervous breakdown. "You know, my strategy has worked so far, and in the last show I was very cautious. It cost me valuable wild cards early on."

Charles asks one last time to be allowed to go through the answers. As he reads out 'Googol,' another cough is heard.

"Chris, I'm going to play!" the major announces. The audience gasps in amazement; Diana can't watch it anymore. She can't remember the last time she had been so tense.

"I'll take googol!"

" Final answer?"

" Final Answer."

The answer is logged. Now there's no way back. Will Charles lose a hefty £468,000 and keep the family's £32,000 curse alive?

Or will his winnings double, and he'll leave the studio a fresh-faced millionaire in minutes?

"Please don't go to commercial now, please don't go to commercial now!" begs Charles, eyes closed, laughing, "please don't!"

Tarrant looks mischievously into Charles' eyes for a moment.

"I'm going to commercial!" he announces, and amid general suffering, urges the audience at home to stay tuned. "This is shaping up to be an epic night," the host dismisses viewers and contestants into the commercial break.

The theme song echoes through the studio, the audience applauds, and the spotlights adjust.

"Welcome back to *Who Wants to Be a Millionaire*," Tarrant greets viewers after the commercials. "Major Charles Ingram came back to us tonight with 4,000 pounds plus a leftover joker and played his way up to 500,000 pounds. On the £1 million question, he initially chose 'Nanomole' but then went back through his options and ultimately chose 'Googol,' mainly for the reason that he'd never heard of it before.

Charles, give me the £500,000 check."

Reluctantly, Ingram follows the instruction and hands the piece of paper to the presenter. The latter tears it up with the words:

"This no longer belongs to you."

Charles takes another deep breath. His wife Diana can hardly wait either. Then Tarrant announces the result.

"You've just won a million pounds!"

Cheering fireworks explode in the studio, and glitter rains from the ceiling. Charles buries his face in his fists and can't believe it.

"You're the most amazing contestant we've ever had!" exclaims Tarrant, beaming with joy, and wraps the major in his arms, "Diana come on down!"

The beaming woman doesn't need to be told twice and immediately descends the steps. When she reaches the middle, she falls into her husband's arms with tears in her eyes. Charles, too, begins to cry with unbridled joy. Meanwhile, Chris Tarrant stands by, beaming all over.

"Come here, Charles!" he says, putting an arm around Charles' shoulder. "I have no idea how you did that!"

He hands the check to the newly minted millionaire and congratulates him again. Then the show's tight schedule presses on, and the Ingrams have to go backstage, where they celebrate their triumph, deeply embraced.

While the new contestants in the selection round fight for the place in the middle, a member of the production team goes to the Ingrams' dressing room and offers the winner a celebratory drink. He declines and explains that he has to work the next day. As the lady leaves the dressing room shortly afterward, she hears what sounds like an excited exchange of words between Charles and Diana through the closed door. In the eyes of the employee, a strange way to celebrate winning a million pounds.

Meanwhile, in the studio, none other than Tecwen Whittock has made it to Chris Tarrant's chair. Contrary to high expectations, he already fails the 8,000-pound question and falls back to 1,000 pounds.

Before Charles and Diana can even leave the premises of Elstree Film & Television Studios, they are searched by production staff, supposedly "as a matter of routine." In fact, however, they are searching for possible evidence of the suspected fraud. However, they do not find anything, which is why the Ingrams are allowed to go home. However, the couple has to leave one thing behind: the one-million-pound check that Charles received from Tarrant. Here, too, the production tries to talk its way out of it by saying that it will take a few days to cash the check by default. In truth, Celador is merely trying to buy time to review the recording in detail.

In the following days, all audio experts evaluate the material and isolate almost 200 coughs that were captured by the microphones on both recording days. Eighteen of these are said to have come from Tecwen Whittock and one from Diana Ingram.

The camera footage also reinforces the producers' suspicions that Charles' game may have been faked: it is usually customary for those accompanying the contestants to keep an eye on their loved ones the entire time or to look at one of the screens hanging in the studio to watch the live taping. Diana, on the other hand, looked in the direction of the selection candidates - where Tecwen Whittock was - conspicuously often during the second day of taping.

The production team decides not to air the show for the time being and refuses to pay out the prize money. Paul Smith delivers the bad news to Charles personally over the phone:

"Mr. Ingram, we don't know each other. But I'm the general manager of Celador. I think I'll get straight to the point: unfortunately, we have to tell you that something seems strange to us after we reviewed the material from last Monday. There seems to have been some irregularities within the program, in which you are significantly involved."

"Oh, good Lord. No!" replies Charles indignantly.

"Further, I must inform you that we have passed the information on to the police. Therefore, for the time being, the show will not be aired, and the check will not be cashed."

In the further course of the conversation, the major rejects all accusations but still shows himself composed. For Celador, this reaction is surprising. The man is about to lose a million pounds and is in the midst of a police investigation - and yet he seems completely unaffected.

True, Charles does not raise his voice on the phone; on paper, however, he fires back with all his might. He not only files a civil suit against Celador but also tries to claim his million-dollar winnings, including 240,000 pounds in legal costs, through the courts. His efforts, however, remain unsuccessful.

Despite his constant protestations that he had not noticed any coughs during the entire program and had certainly not cheated, Charles was arrested together with his wife Diana and Tecwen Whittock on July 31, 2002, and questioned by the police about the accusations. In the process, "Major Fraud," as the press christened Charles, claimed that he knew the answer to every question and did not want to have perceived any coughs. Only on the million-dollar question did he have to draw on his knowledge of physics and mathematics.

Tecwen Whittock defends himself by saying that his coughing during the recording was due to a medically proven combination of asthma, hay fever, and an allergy to dust. Furthermore, he said, it was completely idiotic to want to cheat on the show; after all, one would be surrounded by cameras the entire time. Secretly, he said, he hoped Charles would end the game quickly so he could get his own shot at the 'hot seat.'

When Diana is asked about the call to Whittock after the first recording, she says she just wanted to wish him "good luck." The conversation, she says, lasted about five minutes - "far too short" to be able to devise a plan of such substance.

Her husband had not known about this phone call and had expressed dismay when he learned about it.

Moreover, in the eyes of the defendants, it would speak for itself that the alleged answer-giver failed even the 8,000-pound question. How likely is it that, while he knew every answer in Charles' game, he himself didn't have a clue on his own turn? Might the accompanying nervousness in the guessing chair have prevented him from thinking rationally?

"The jury is now faced with a 50-50 question," the prosecutor chortles, turning off the tube TV. "Guilty or not guilty?"

It is March 03, 2003, at Southwark Crown Court, London. The first day of the trial of Charles and Diana Ingram and Tecwen Whittock. All three are accused of cheating on the quiz show '*Who Wants to Be a Millionaire.*' In the eyes of the plaintiffs, the major had a plan to obtain a large sum of money in order to pay off his debt of 50,000 pounds (60000 USD). The reason for this assumption is the coughs registered during the recording from the direction of the candidate Tecwen Whittock. Strangely enough, these were always heard when Ingram tended to give a wrong answer. Several times one could reconstruct by means of the video tapes that these coughs led to sudden U-turns of the candidate on the council chair.

Prosecutors believe the Ingrams and Whittock spoke regularly on the phone for several months before the taping but deliberately ignored each other in the studio so as not to arouse suspicion. The defendants claim they never met or spoke to each other.

The vibrating pager theory is also revisited. Did Charles and Diana possibly intend this method to cheat on the first day of recording and ultimately consider it too risky? In any case, there is no evidence for this.

After the trial had to be interrupted for two days due to uncontrollable coughing fits on the part of the jury, the court finally sentences Charles and Diana Ingram to eighteen months probation in mid-April 2003. In addition, they must pay a fine of 20000 USD each and a contribution to legal costs of 15,000 USD each. Tecwen Whittock receives one year's probation and a fine of 10,000 pounds, including a contribution to legal costs of 10,000 USD. For all three convicts, the probation period is set at two years.

At the end of the trial, the judge reveals starkly that he only refrained from imposing a prison sentence so as not to separate the parents from their three children. In his eyes, the Ingrams performed a "shabby schoolboy trick."

As a result of losing the case, 'Major Fraud' must leave the Army at the end of August. Despite his early retirement, however, he is allowed to keep his rank as well as his pension entitlement.

A few months later, Charles is on trial again. This time he is charged with insurance fraud amounting to 35,000 USD after antique furniture was allegedly stolen from his house. The jury finds him guilty in this case as well.

Although the couple had hoped for a ray of hope on the horizon after the strain of the two trials, the Ingram family is instead moving from the frying pan into the fire. The fines worsen their financial situation so drastically that they go bankrupt in October 2004. They, therefore, try to negotiate a total of 70,000 USD in fines down to 35,000 USD. This is granted to them, although the judge suspects that Charles and Diana also faked their precarious financial situation in order to escape the high sum.

The family is subjected to more than 60 attacks, aggression, and vandalism over five years. Among them, teenagers break into their garden and throw stones through three windows of the family home; two weeks later, a bag of vomit suddenly smashes against the wall of the house.

"We've found bolts and nails set up in the house driveway, the word 'scam' has been scratched into the paint of our car, and someone regularly emptied their garbage can in our backyard," Charles recounted in a 2007 interview with the Daily Mail. "Last year, one of our dogs was abused by a group of teenagers and died as a result. My wife is constantly surrounded by adolescents shouting 'cheating bitch' at her."

Not even family outings, such as to the movies, are no longer possible, she says, because people are constantly coughing at them.

On April 30, 2006, these daily harassments finally reach their peak: Charles is on his daily jog when he approaches a group of six children. A 13-year-old boy gets in his way and coughs so loudly in Charles' face that spit lands on his lips. The major then loses his temper, grabs the boy by the collar, and yells:

"You do that again; you'll bitterly regret it!"

The boy then calls the police and reports being attacked by Ingram and pushed against a fence. Although he later admits to exaggerating the story somewhat, Charles is found guilty of assault. The new conviction means that he now has to leave the Army for good, losing his pension entitlements as well as his title. The Ingram family now seems to have reached rock bottom. Despair and helplessness have already eaten into daily life to such an extent that Charles is toying with the idea of putting an end to his life. With forty pills in one hand and a glass of water in the other, he sits up in bed one evening around 10:00 p.m. and finds himself only moments away from suicide. But the vibrating of his cell phone thwarts his plan. A text message from his daughters appears on the screen: *'We all believe in you, Dad."*

Charles became unemployed as a result of the scandal on '*Who Wants to Be a Millionaire.*' So he spends most of his time fixing computers and writing novels. His first book, *'The Network,'* was published in April 2006, and the second, *'Deep Siege,'* in October 2007. His wife Diana earns her money by selling jewelry she makes herself. In addition, the couple occasionally guest stars in reality formats on television, such as *'Celebrity Poker Club'* or *'Celebrity wife swap.'* It may not be what they wanted from their lives after appearing on *'Who Wants to Be a Millionaire,'* but at least they earn their money in an honest way.

As the first decade of the 2000s comes to an end, peace gradually returns, and public interest in the family ebbs. The last time Charles makes headlines is in 2010 when he accidentally slips on a rotten apple in his backyard, and his foot gets caught under the lawnmower. In the process, he cuts off two and a half toes.

Although the station initially decided not to air the episode about "*Major Fraud,*" they did make up for it in the spring of 2003. A television documentary was then shown under the title 'Millionaire: A Major Fraud,' with which ITV was able to achieve an audience rating of 17 million viewers. The documentary features interviews with contestants, production staff, and presenter Chris Tarrant. The latter says in the film that he did not hear a single suspicious cough during the entire recording.

Is Charles possibly innocent after all? He and his wife, at any rate, maintain their innocence to this day and are looking for opportunities to appeal. Until then, for now, the same question that viewers are asked at the beginning of the film 'Slumdog Millionaire' remains:

Major Charles Ingram is one question away from becoming a millionaire. How did he do it?

    A: He cheated
    B: He got lucky
    C: He is a genius
    D: It was fate

LIES ARE LIKE AN UNSTABLE HOUSE OF CARDS - TAKE ONE WRONG CARD OUT OF THE STRUCTURE AND EVERYTHING COLLAPSES.

- Steffi (Podcast: Von Mord und Todschlag
(Of murder and mayhem)) -

CHAPTER 6

THE HOUSE OF CARDS

It's July 27, 2008, when Clark chooses the wrong card. The little blonde girl reaches for her father's hand and smiles at him. After her parents' difficult divorce, the 7-year-old hasn't seen her dad for some time. Her mother had moved to London, more than 5,000 kilometers away, together with their daughter.

The 47-year-old is walking through Boston's Back Bay neighborhood with his little daughter, whom he affectionately calls "Snooks." They are on their way to the oldest city park in the United States - Boston Common. Here, they want to spend their little time together and enjoy the warm summer sun. Clark looks at his little "Snooks," lost in thought. After the separation from his wife, he no longer has custody of the daughter they share, and the rare meetings with the 7-year-old are not allowed to take place without supervision - so Clark agreed with his ex-wife. That's why a bored social worker is now strolling behind father and daughter. As the trio turns a corner, the 47-year-old notices nervousness slowly rising in him. His heart begins to race; his hands are wet with sweat. He can make out a black car at the end of the street. Clark quickens his gait so that the 7-year-old almost has to run to keep up with her dad. When the father and daughter almost arrive at the dark car with the running engine, Clark decisively turns to face the social worker hurrying behind. He brings down the surprised man with a firm shove to the chest. Then the 47-year-old grabs little "Snooks," yanks open the rear door of the black car, shoves his daughter into the back seat, and hastily gets into the car as well before slamming the door noisily. The social worker uses a few seconds to catch his breath and rushes to the vehicle. He reaches for the door handle as Clark tells the driver to drive off; he immediately presses the gas pedal. With screeching tires, the car shoots off and drags the social worker behind it for a few more meters until he plucks up the courage to let go of the door handle and hits the asphalt hard. Completely exhausted, the man remains lying on the road.

On February 21, 1961, a little boy was born in the Bavarian community of Siegsdorf in the district of Traunstein. The Gerhartsreiter couple names their son Christian Karl. He is still a toddler when mother Irmgard is already pregnant with her second child. Father Simon served in World War II and returned home with lung disease. Throughout his life, the former soldier had trouble breathing and could no longer do any heavy work. The family man spends his days capturing landscapes in oil paintings. But the painter is not very successful and earns only a little money with his art - at least, it is not enough to support his wife and two sons. Mother Irmgard is a gifted seamstress and thus improves the empty family coffers. No matter whether a pair of trousers needs to be let out or a dirndl mended - the villagers place their garments in the trusting hands of Frau Gerhartsreiter. Perhaps that's why Christian and Alexander are always dressed a little more fashionably than the other village children.

Even in kindergarten, Christian is more rebellious than his peers. At school, he provokes his classmates at every possible opportunity, thus ensuring that he does not make any friends. He often comes across as an unpleasant know-it-all to his peers. The student does not stop at teachers either: the boy is in the fifth grade when he blows pepper into his teacher's eyes. Early on, Christian fiddles around with an air rifle until, one day; he shatters the valuable stained-glass window of the village church. No one knows where the student got the weapon. Although the teenager brags to his classmates about his father's supposedly huge arsenal of weapons, when the other boys urge him to show them the collection, he plays evasive.

When Christian is bored, he invents false identities here and there. Slipping into other roles is something the boy finds very easy, perhaps also because he gets into the habit of speaking High German instead of Bavarian at an early age. Thus, the teenager once calls the car registration office. In a disguised, deep voice, he brazenly tells the official on the other end of the line that he is a millionaire from Holland and wants to register his two newly purchased Rolls-Royces. He proudly tells his classmates that the servant bought his tall tale without hesitation.

The boy is known for inventing abstruse stories. One day, for example, he apologizes to his teacher for being late to class with the excuse that he overslept only because his alarm clock exploded.

While his peers spend their free time together and enjoy the hot summer at nearby Lake Chiemsee, the solitary Christian squats alone in his father's workshop, tinkering with radios and radio sets, he dreams of emigrating to America one day. A country that is said to offer unlimited opportunities. He feels constricted by the idyllic Bavarian countryside. Christian soaks up all the influences that slowly spill over from the other continent to Germany. The boy loves movies set in the USA. That's when he can dream of himself in an American suburb with white wooden houses, well-kept front gardens, and wide, tree-lined streets.

At the age of 18, Christian is liable for military service. But the young man, always mindful of his lung-diseased father, is almost panic-stricken about joining the Bundeswehr. The teenager sees a chance to make his dream come true and escape the draft on a train ride. There he meets the American couple Elmer and Jean Kelln from Berlin, a small town in Connecticut. At the end of a little chat, they exchange addresses with their travel acquaintance. Christian could visit them when he was in the US. Despite their limited financial means, his parents finance the trip for him - without suspecting that they would never see their son again.

Alexander is not surprised that his big brother leaves home when he is still a teenager. Christian has always said that he wants to become famous. However, the runaway does not yet know what he wants to do when he boards a plane to the USA in 1978.

The American couple Kelln is initially at a loss as to what to do with the young German, who one day appears on their doorstep with his suitcases packed. The emigrant can stay with the Kellns for a short time - but this is not a permanent situation. Elmer and Jean place ads in a local newspaper looking for a host family for Christian.

One of the ads was answered by the Savio family. They had already hosted an exchange student from France the year before and had a good experience. The Savios' house is small and modestly furnished, but they offer the German to sleep on their sofa. In August 1980, Christian Karl Gerhartsreiter arrives at the door of the Italian family, who, like the Kellns, live in Connecticut's Berlin. However, he introduces himself with the surname Reiter - this is easier to pronounce for the Americans, he explains. He asks his new host family to call him "Chris.

Mother Gwen Savios examines the young man from top to bottom, who wears tops and pants that are far too tight for her taste. The German is small and lanky in stature - he measures less than 5'5". Despite his age, the teenager has short brown hair and an already pronounced receding hairline. His nose looks too big for his square face above his narrow lips. Black horn-rimmed glasses give the 19-year-old an intellectual edge. The young man speaks fluent English, albeit with a strong German accent.

The houseguest quickly settles in with the Savios and is enthusiastic about the American lifestyle. Chris is fascinated by the colorful Ford Mustangs with their long hoods. His favorite snack is cookies consisting of two choux pastry cookies held together by a sweet milk cream filling.

Christian also works hard on his English. He lets his counterpart improve until he pronounces the corresponding vocabulary word without an accent.

His host family has a son who is about the same age as Chris. Edward, later a successful book and screenwriter, takes the German with him whenever he goes out with his friends. But Chris soon lets on that he doesn't feel like it at all - he's picky when it comes to who he spends his free time with. The teenager prefers to talk to adults.

The two boys go to a high school in Berlin. Here there is a recording studio and a small radio station, where Chris spends most of his time after school from then on. The German exchange student even gets a broadcasting slot where he sends classical music into the ether every evening. The boss of the small radio station is thrilled when the young German announces a piece by Beethoven with his European accent.

After Chris's first radio broadcast, the school principal even calls him and congratulates his student on the successful start.

Meanwhile, the Savios' enthusiasm for their houseguest continues to wane. After a short time, there is no trace of the obliging and friendly young man. Instead, a loutish teenager now sits on their couch and stares at the TV while he shoos Mother Gwen into doing his dirty laundry and complains about how awful she is at cooking. At home in Bavaria, he says, everything is much fancier and more distinguished; his father is an important industrialist. The hired house staff would never have dared to serve Chris and his family such slop as he now has to eat at the Savios'.

In January 1981, the host family finally had enough. They throw Gerhartsreiter out the door. The school principal tries to find a new place for the German exchange student to stay. The dedicated man quickly finds what he is looking for: the school's librarian offers to let Chris stay with her. She knows the homeless boy, who often sits with her in the library and browses through various publications. In addition, the woman has learned the German language. That was ages ago, but somehow it makes her feel connected to the teenager.

The librarian takes great care of the German. She washes his clothes, cooks, and eats dinner with him. Chris tells the woman a different story from the Savios: his father is a scientist, and his mother is a concert pianist.

But even this living arrangement does not last long. After just two months, things fall apart when Chris refuses to pay his phone bill. In desperation, the librarian turns to the school principal. He orders his student to pay the bill. But he is no longer allowed to live with the woman.

Chris does not finish school in Berlin, Connecticut. There is no evidence that Gerhartsreiter once attended classes here. Only in the library is a yearbook from 1979, in which the student signed his name in scrawling script on page two. Since he didn't attend the school until 1981, there wasn't even a photo of him in the issue.

After being kicked out by the school librarian, Chris leaves Connecticut. He tells his former schoolmates that he wants to go to California, almost 5,000 kilometers away, to make a name for himself in the film business. In fact, however, he first moves to Wisconsin, only 1600 kilometers away from Connecticut.

Here he introduces himself to new acquaintances as Christopher Kenneth Gerhart. The 19-year-old enrolls at the University of Milwaukee-Wisconsin to learn the art of acting. It is not known if he studied at the academy and, if so, for how long. However, it appears that, from the start, Gerhartsreiter did not intend to stay in the city for too long.

Just one day before his 20th birthday, the young man married Amy Jersild Duhnke, two years his senior, in Madison, 130 kilometers from Milwaukee. Before the civil ceremony, the young people may have known each other for only a few weeks. One suspects that the 20-year-old got the young woman by a feint to agree to marry him. He is said to have made her believe that, because of the Cold War, he would be drafted into the military and sent to the front in Russia if he returned to West Germany. Only a "green card," a document officially allowing him to live and work in the US, could get him out of trouble. So, the 22-year-old must have been persuaded to marry the man from Germany, who was almost a stranger to her. On the day of the wedding, Amy realizes that Gerhartsreiter is not only, but exclusively, interested in the green card. Her newlywed husband makes a run for it. The abandoned wife does not file for divorce until 1992, a full eleven years after the wedding. A strange story. I wonder if Amy really had no idea what Chris was about before the wedding. Some claim he paid her money to enter into a sham marriage with him. The now 63-year-old ex-wife does not comment on this publicly.

With the green card in his pocket, Gerhartsreiter can finally set off for California, some 3,200 kilometers from Madison. How he earns his living during this time and how he pays for the expensive trips across the country cannot be reconstructed. But it is said that his parents finance the expensive pleasure. But can this be his only source of income? After all, Simon and Irmgard Gerhartsreiter live very modestly and have no great wealth. It is said that the Germans often wandered through the busy streets of noble cities, closely observing privileged people, and then imitating their behavior. In this way, the man, who was always neatly dressed, managed to curry favor with single, mostly older, but always well-off women. Dazzled by his charm and intellect, the ladies would have flattered Chris and also lent him sums of money from time to time.

With high-quality business cards decorated with a family coat of arms and alleged verification from the English royal family, Gerhartsreiter henceforth passes himself off as a nobleman.

In 1984, now under the name Christopher Chichester, he meets the elderly and single Didi Sohus. The lady lives in a splendid house with a large estate in San Marino, a noble suburb of Los Angeles. Thanks to the charm of the alleged English nobleman, Didi offers him to stay in her guest house.

The 23-year-old Chichester keeps his landlady company and helps her with chores she can no longer do herself. Didi hires the young man as a domestic helper - for the first time, Chichester earns his own money. Soon he is irreplaceable for Didi. She trusts the young man. That is why she grants him unrestricted access to her bank account.

Chichester quickly settles into life in San Marino. He joins the Rotary Club, regularly attends the local church, and gets involved in charitable causes. And he tries to advance his acting career - always with Hollywood in mind. He enrolls at the University of California in Los Angeles to get closer to his dream. The lie that he is a producer at the English television station BBC secures him a place in one of the university's best film classes. Here he even meets the famous producer Steven Spielberg at a workshop. Everything goes as the now 24-year-old imagines - until Didi's adopted son John and his wife Linda arrive on the doorstep one day. The young couple moves into Didi's big house, which doesn't suit Chichester at all. He has already imagined what he would do with all the money when Didi passes away one day. John and Linda, however, are now throwing a spanner in the works - meaning that there would be nothing left for Chichester after Didi Sohus' death.

The 24-year-old devises a diabolical plan. How exactly he carries out his plan is not known to this day. The only thing that is certain is that one day he smashes John's skull with a bludgeoning weapon, possibly a baseball bat. He buries the dead man's body unobserved in Didi's garden. A friend of Chichester's at the time believes he must have felt invincible to his unsuspecting guests. He may even have felt a diabolical joy that they were dancing on his victim's grave.

Of course, Didi, neighbors, acquaintances, and friends notice that John and Linda disappeared one day. Chichester explains that the young couple inexplicably ran away. He persuades old Didi that her children have abandoned her. But when Linda's sister files a missing person's report, Gerhartsreiter gets a little too hot under the collar. He would rather give up the old lady's inheritance than end up in prison for murder.

With John and Linda's pickup, Gerhartsreiter sets off for Greenwich, California. "Christopher Crowe," as he now calls himself, is an alleged television producer from Los Angeles. He gets a job at a brokerage firm. But he is soon summarily dismissed when his employer discovers that Crowe has not given his social security number but that of the notorious serial killer David Berkowitz. When Gerhartsreiter learns that the police are looking for him in connection with the disappearance of John and Linda Sohus, he takes off in a cloak-and-dagger operation. The fugitive is aware that his disappearance after the disappearance of the couple has put him in the focus of the investigators. But he can't take that into account now.

The next time Christian Gerhartsreiter shows his face is in New York in 1987 when he goes underground in Manhattan - the district where power and money are based. With his fairy tale of coming from an English aristocratic family, the now 26-year-old landed a job in the US offices of the securities firm Nikko Securities on Wall Street. His annual salary is an estimated 150,000 US dollars - and he's completely clueless about what he's actually doing. But if there's one thing Gerhartsreiter knows how to do, it's keeping up appearances. His employees quickly realize, however, that the young Crowe doesn't have a clue. But what are they to do? The manager is known to be dazzled by blue-blooded pedigree instead of checking references.

But at some point, it seems to become clear that something can't be right with Crowe because he is fired. But Gerhartsreiter is not discouraged by this. He manages to get himself a responsible position at another investment firm in Manhattan. But only shortly after taking the job, he quits again. His parents had been killed in Afghanistan, and he now had to take care of the estate. Then he disappears. The quick disappearance is probably due to Gerhartsreiter's suspicion that the police are hot on his heels because of the Sohus couple's missing persons case. Only a short time after he disappeared, the officers are standing in the office of his last place of work - but there is no trace of Crow far and wide.

Gerhartsreiter decides to give up the identity of Christopher Crowe and henceforth call himself "James Frederick Mills Clark Rockefeller" - an alleged member of one of the wealthiest and most influential families in the world.

The young man, who can only be addressed by his last first name, "Clark," regularly visits St. Thomas Church. This is where New York's high society worships. Gerhartsreiter is now 32 years old when the pretty Sandra Boss catches his eye at one of the services. They strike up a conversation. Rockefeller learns that the young woman with the petite face is the daughter of a Boeing engineer and is just graduating from Harvard Business School.

Sandra is a quiet, reserved, but very determined person. She has many suitors. Nevertheless, she decides to enter into a relationship with the small, lanky Rockefeller, who apparently doesn't have as great a fortune as he always pretends. When the young couple goes out to dinner, Sandra is the one who always has to pull out her wallet to settle the bill. But friends later say that the attractive woman falls in love with the unassuming man because he makes her laugh. Besides, the sophisticated man is very charming. Sandra trusts him and feels sorry for him when he tearfully tells her that he was just a little boy when his parents were killed in a car accident. He sticks to that story in the years that follow. When Rockefeller proposes to Sandra, she says "yes" without hesitation. At the age of 34, the con man thus marries for a second time in 1995. This time according to the customs of the "Religious Society of Friends,"; these are also derisively referred to as "Quakers." However, the Quaker ceremony has no legal force. Gerhartsreiter must have been very pleased about this - after all, he did not have any papers with which he could identify himself to state authorities as Rockefeller. The young couple settles in New York. The newly married Sandra gets a job as a well-paid executive at McKinsey, a global management consulting firm.

Meanwhile, a pit for a swimming pool is to be dug on Didi Sohus' former property. In the process, the construction workers make a gruesome discovery. While excavating the soil, the men come across a skeleton wrapped in plastic bags. They inform the police about their shocking find. Forensic investigators discover, in addition to the bones, the remains of a flannel shirt and blue jeans - typical clothing that the missing John Sohus always wore. Forensic experts determine that the man was killed with two firm blows to the head and at least six strokes of a knife before his body was cut into three pieces. Forensic experts are able to visualize a pool of blood in the mansion's guest house using a chemical called "luminol." However, it is expected to take until 2010 before the bones can be attributed to John Sohus without a doubt.

While the investigators in San Marino are working flat out on the case of the skeleton they found, Sandra's husband turns out to be a rotten egg. If he previously carried her in his hands and saw it as his main job to take care of her in a caring way, he turns out to be more and more of a true domestic tyrant. Although Sandra is the only one earning money, it is Gerhartsreiter who seizes control of the finances. The unequal couple quarrels more and more often. Rockefeller had psychologically abused her, the woman later recounts.

Although there is a suspicion that Sandra Boss could be a confidant in Gerhartsreiter's swindle, the woman claims not to have suspected anything. Perhaps she is also ashamed of having allowed herself to be blinded in this way - after all, she is one of the country's top managers. Gerhartsreiter also takes great pains to hide his true identity from Sandra. For example, he asks her to file her tax return as an individual. To keep up appearances, Gerhartsreiter hires an accountant after the marriage to do the tax return for the couple. Only later does Sandra learn that her husband told the accountant that the two were supposedly siblings.

For this reason, she says, the accountant continued to file the tax returns individually. Still, there are no documents to prove that Clark Rockefeller is really who he says he is. This is one of many inconsistencies of the impostor, which cannot be cleared up even later.

On May 24, 2001, Sandra and Clark's only daughter is born. They name the little girl Reigh Storrow Rockefeller. The child is the pride and joy of her father, who is now 40 years old. His new mission in life is to sacrificially care for his daughter, whom he affectionately calls "Snooks." Some say he nurtured the little girl, teaching her to read and do fractions at an early age. Others, however, believe Rockefeller's nurturing was much more like dressage. You rarely see Rockefeller alone now - he usually has the bright-eyed Reigh with him. Sometimes he holds the little blonde girl by her tiny hand; sometimes, she sits on her father's shoulders. Clark spends most of his time taking care of his daughter. Sandra has to work a lot in her position and is not at home most of the day.

The small family initially moves to the state of New Hampshire. But as Reigh's enrollment in school approaches, Sandra pushes to relocate to Boston, about 90 kilometers away. This is where she has her office. At first, Clark resists the move but then relents. In the fall of 2006, the Rockefellers move into a townhouse that has three floors.

Clark quickly settles into his new home and is soon a respected member of the community. But behind the noble facade of the townhouse, the marriage begins to crumble more and more. Just a few months after the move, Sandra files for divorce. Another mystery of the story. After all, there is no marriage certificate. Even how the final separation comes about is supposed to remain hidden from the public. The Rockefellers make sure that the file about their divorce remains sealed. There are rumors that Sandra asked her husband to reveal his true identity after hiring a private investigator. However, the alleged Rockefeller had flatly refused to reveal anything about his true origins. What is certain is that Sandra will pay Gerhartsreiter $800,000 in the divorce. He also receives two cars, her engagement ring, and an expensive dress he once bought her. In return, she gets sole custody of their six-year-old daughter, allowing Clark Rockefeller to escape "due diligence," a careful analysis of a person. For Rockefeller, this would have meant revealing his sham identity.

From then on, little Reigh bears the surname Boss. Her mother moves to England with the girl, leaving Clark frustrated in the Boston townhouse. He is now only allowed to see his beloved daughter, as per the agreement, three times a year under supervision and regrets ever having entered into the deal with his ex-wife. The failed con man misses his little Snooks. Hatred for Sandra and an agonizing longing for his only child cloud the con man's senses. For decades he has been able to successfully conceal his true identity. Carefully he laid card upon card and thus kept up a splendid-looking structure of lies. But now the 47-year-old Gerhartsreiter is carefully planning the kidnapping of his daughter - and thus pulls the very pillar out of the construction that will cause the house of cards to collapse.

Gerhartsreiter closes his eyes and takes a deep breath. He has managed to lose the social worker who, according to a court order, is supposed to supervise the meetings with his daughter. The 47-year-old reaches for Snooks' hand; the little girl sits next to him in the back seat of the black getaway car. The driver of the car doesn't know that he is involved in a child abduction at that very moment. "Clark Rockefeller" merely informed him that he had to travel to an important meeting. For some time, however, he had been followed by a stranger whom he had to lose beforehand. Therefore, he asked his acquaintance to wait for him and his daughter at the street corner with the engine running. Gerhartsreiter's thin lips twisted into a smile. His plan seems to be working. He has thought everything through to the last detail.

Gerhartsreiter bought an old carriage house through a realtor in Baltimore, Maryland, about 650 kilometers from Boston. The rooms of the house are only sparsely furnished; packed moving boxes are still standing around everywhere. Gerhartsreiter keeps the curtains drawn. There is only a small rice stove in the kitchen. This is how he will spend the next few days living in the hideout with his young daughter. He pays 450,000 US dollars for the nondescript brick cottage - for 10,000 US dollars, he buys a catamaran, which he pays for in cash. What will future life be like with his kidnapped daughter? How will he explain the long flight to Baltimore to the girl? What does the con man say when his little Snooks asks for her mommy?

Meanwhile, Sandra Boss is nearly sick with worry for her young daughter. Authorities immediately initiate elaborate search efforts; the image of Clark Rockefeller flickers across television screens across the country with a notice that the man is wanted for child abduction. The realtor recognizes the wanted man - but he introduced himself to her as Chip Smith. The charming man told her that he wanted to move from Chile to Baltimore with his daughter. She immediately picks up the phone and alerts the police.

The officers immediately begin planning their response. On August 02, 2008, six days after the little girl's abduction, dozens of plainclothes officers surround the carriage house where they suspect Clark Rockefeller is staying. But they don't want to storm the building - fearing they might endanger Reigh.

Instead, they set a trap for Gerhartsreiter. They ask the manager of the harbor where the catamaran of the wanted man is moored to call the man. He is to tell him that water is entering the barge. "I'll be right there," Gerhartsreiter replies. After hanging up the phone, he slips on his shoes, leaves the house, and wants to go to the harbor. This is what the officers have been waiting for. They seize him as soon as the man steps out of the door. The plainclothesmen rush Gerhartsreiter and pull him to the ground to handcuff him. Then the policemen go into the small house, take out the completely frightened seven-year-old girl and bring her to her mother. Sandra is overjoyed to finally be able to hold her daughter again.

The arrested man is remanded in custody. A number of witnesses come forward to report the identities under which they know the impostor. Statement after statement fit together like pieces of a puzzle and put the investigators on the right track. They obtain the immigration file of the German Christian Gerhartsreiter and carry out elaborate fingerprint analyses, at the end of which the suspicion about the true identity of the impostor is confirmed.

On June 12, 2009, the court announces the jury's verdict: Gerhartsreiter was guilty of child abduction as well as assault with a dangerous weapon when he ordered the driver of the getaway vehicle to drive on, even though the social worker was holding onto the car's door handle. The judge will impose a prison sentence for kidnapping Reigh of four to five years. The defendant gets up to three years on top for dangerous bodily harm.

In March 2011, the prosecution charges Gerhartsreiter with the murder of John Sohus. The jury also finds him guilty on that count, so the judge imposes a prison sentence of 27 years to life. The convicted man appeals - with moderate success. His sentence is changed to 26 years to life.

In 2022, Christian Gerhartsreiter, now 61, is serving his sentence in San Quentin, California's oldest state prison. The con man denies to this day that he committed the murder of John Sohus and had anything to do with Linda's disappearance. Therefore, he appealed twice against the sentences passed - both times, the judiciary rejected his request. With a lot of goodwill on the part of the authorities, Gerhartsreiter could be released on parole in 2029. The man would then be 68 years old.

He has had no contact with his family since 1985. Father Simon died in September 2003. It is not known whether Mother Irmgard is still alive; she would have been well over 90 years old this year. The last time she appears in public is shortly after her 80th birthday. Confronted with a photo of her son, she says the astonishing sentence for a mother: "He died for me years ago." Alexander, too, wants nothing more to do with his older brother.

Didi Sohus never got over the sudden disappearance of her adopted son. She felt abandoned. The old, frail woman died in February 1988, never knowing what fate befell her son and that he had not left Didi voluntarily.

But what happened to John's wife, Linda? Some believe that she went on the run with Chichester; others believe that she, too, at the same time as her husband, was murdered by the German impostor. Whatever really happened, the fact is that Linda was never seen again. Things have been quiet around Sandra Boss and her daughter Reigh, now a young adult woman of 21. After the then 7-year-old girl was freed from the coachman's house, she and her mother flew back to London, where they lead a low-key life. The impostor's ex-wife is ashamed that she fell for his tall tales. Now 63, she tries to put the past behind her and build a new life. But not in the form of a shaky house of cards.

*Silent, without splendor, but sure
to be noticed:
Thus Prince and Dogg' walk in
their strength.
In silk and bells, flaunting and
barking and cursing with clamor
The squire and his pooch.*

- Johann Heinrich Voß (1751–1826),
German poet and translator –

CHAPTER 7

PRINCE DUBAI

S outhern music plays in the background as the user named "princedubai_07" opens the Instagram app on his smartphone and begins recording a video for his followers.

"You know it," he says in his husky voice reminiscent of Donald Trump, "we closed the entire pool so the boss can swim undisturbed."

Meanwhile, he pans across the deserted pool area. The night sky is black, the turquoise water blue, and the surrounding lounge chairs are bathed in the orange light of spotlights mounted on the palm trees.

"Here chills Foxy ...". A black Chihuahua with white paws comes into the picture. He is lying on a cushion, watching his owner with an interested expression. "There's my Louis Vuitton bag ..."

The man points the camera at the deck chair standing next to Foxy, where a dark brown leather bag with beige handles is placed.

"That's what bosses do," he says, continuing to pan the cell phone camera around. The soft lapping of water can be heard in the background.

"We've closed the entire pool area ...," he repeats, " ... so that we can ..."

He strides through the water toward the edge of the pool. There stands a tray with a pitcher and two glasses. The contents are cloudy, with mint and lemon slices floating on the surface.

"... enjoy an apple mojito under the palm trees ..."

He grabs one of the glasses and sips.

"Cheers everyone! Enjoy life, do yourselves some favors, and treat yourselves the way you deserve."

With these words ends the video that "princedubai_07" posted online on June 21, 2017, with the succinct description "Chilling." Who exactly is behind the username is not revealed. All it shows is an apparent life of luxury with fat bling, luxurious food, private jets, and expensive hotels.

However, the true identity of "princedubais" is not entirely unknown. A look at the comments section of his posts shows that users don't really trust the alleged origin of his extravagant lifestyle. And there is a reason for this, for which we have to scroll back to 1970 South America.

At that time, Colombia is a country full of political instability and social unrest. Drug-related crime is increasing dramatically, and violent excesses are becoming more frequent, especially in rural areas. In the midst of these difficult times, José Moreno was born in the capital Bogotá. When his two brothers are born a few years later, the boy's father decides to take a cruel step: since the family is too poor to support three children, he kills his youngest son, which, for unknown reasons, forces José and his brother Daniel to live a hard life on the streets of Bogotá from now on.

To keep himself and Daniel alive, José, just five years old at the time, steals food and looks for safe places to sleep for himself and his brother, who is two years younger. It is even said that he sold his virginity to grown men for survival.

In 1977, the boys' helplessness, as well as their merciless life on the streets, comes to an end when James and Nancy Gignac, a couple from Michigan, some 4,500 kilometers away, adopt the two and bring them to the United States. Although José and Daniel now live in a better environment, the suffering and scars from Colombia have burned deep into their flesh.

When 7-year-old José Moreno, now going by the name Anthony Enrique Gignac, first sets foot on American soil, he doesn't speak a word of English. In addition to the national language, he also learns another dialect - that of lies. In the second grade, for example, he tells his classmates that his biological father is the famous actor Dom DeLuise and that his mother owns the famous Grand Hotel on Mackinac Island.

As Anthony enters sixth grade and puberty gradually takes control of his body, his adoptive mother, Nancy, gets a call one day. On the other end of the line, a Mercedes Benz car dealer answers, telling her that her new car is waiting for her. Nancy is flabbergasted and claims that she didn't order a car, so she confronts her sons. It turns out that Anthony presented himself to the gullible dealer as an alleged Saudi prince, had himself driven around in the Mercedes for a test drive, and had the car prepared for the purchase. His father, the King of Saudi Arabia, would cover the cost.

This behavior has resulted in Nancy and James sending their oldest son to a camp for troubled youth for therapy. They hope he can overcome the dark years in Colombia there and better integrate into American society without bragging about tall tales. In addition, Anthony is panic-stricken, and the people close to his heart will leave him, one of the psychological consequences of his time on the streets.

In 1985, this fear is put to the test. The rioter is just entering the eighth grade when his adoptive parents divorce. Anthony and his brother now have the choice of who they want to stay with from now on. While Anthony chooses his mother, brother Daniel prefers to move in with his father, James. It is the first time the close-knit sibling couple is torn apart, resulting in further psychological stress for Anthony.

In the weeks that follow, these become so bad that Nancy doesn't know what to do and sends her adopted son to a psychiatric hospital, where he stays for a year. He is then transferred to a transitional facility but runs away from there at the age of 17. Now he is completely on his own, believing his adoptive mother has abandoned him.

Sometime later, he meets an Arab family in Michigan and introduces himself to them as "Prince Adnan Khashoggi." He claims that his father, the king of Saudi Arabia, would be "very angry" if they did not take him in. Worried about this threat, the family bows to his will and grants Anthony a new shelter. No one questions why the Saudi Arabian prince looks like a Latino.

Two months later, Anthony travels to Los Angeles, where he begins to experiment with his Middle Eastern identity. As "Prince Khalid bin Al Saud," he forges an identity card for himself and uses it to his advantage. In this way, he is able to claim to be part of the Saudi dynasty as an employee of the "Saks fifth Avenue" store, whereupon he is allowed to use the family's debit account when paying for his products. When Anthony leaves the store, his suitcase contains items totaling $11,000. On the same day, he repeats the scam at another store, spending another $18,000.

During his stay in LA, the fake prince also uses stolen credit cards to buy expensive limousines, hotel rooms, and jewelry. However, it is not long before he is caught, arrested, and put behind bars for two years. The American press, therefore, gives him the title "Prince fraud."

After his stay in prison, Anthony initially flees California but returns to Los Angeles a short time later. He was served a taste of the extravagant lifestyle and is hungry for more. Every time he entered the hotel lobby, he was addressed as "royalty" - a great feeling. He, who spent the first years of his life on the streets of Colombia, stealing food to survive, is now a part of high society. The fact that his illegal methods could have consequences at some point - Anthony doesn't think about that. For him, the only thing that counts is the greed for power, to be able to do anything he likes.

In July 1991, Anthony takes a room in the "Beverly Wilshire" hotel in Los Angeles. After spending over 3,000 dollars on food and his room, he leaves the hotel after only four days. And he did so without paying a single cent. In addition, he squanders more than 70,000 dollars on limousine services. He is comfortably driven around in expensive cars and enjoys his non-existent wealth. However, he can't enjoy it for very long because Anthony is arrested again due to the unpaid hotel bills. At the subsequent trial, he pleads for acquittal; whether he gets it or has to go to prison is not known. A year later, however, he was put behind bars for 53 days after living out his extravagant lifestyle at the Ritz-Carlton Hotel, again without paying.

Following this prison sentence, the self-proclaimed and otherwise self-assured prince is in despair. Should he really spend his life serving a prison sentence every few years? To get his thoughts in order, Anthony travels to Hawaii, where he swindles a couple out of $20,000 to pay off his outstanding bills. Shortly after, however, he returns to the mainland right away and, after a small stopover in Michigan, heads to Florida in 1993. The state is notorious for the scams some people run there. Anthony, too, immediately falls under its spell and fulfills a dream: to visit Disneyland one day.

At the "Walt Disney Grand Floridian Beach Resort," he receives a bill amounting to 14,000 dollars. But once again, the young man does not intend to pay the amount. Although he only receives a suspended sentence for this offense, fate pays him back less than a month later in Miami. After one of his infamous shopping trips on December 30, 1993, he, as an alleged member of the royal family of Saudi Arabia, invites two men unknown to him so far to celebrate in his penthouse in the Grand Bay Hotel in Miami. Once there, Anthony's newfound acquaintances are amazed at his possessions and seize the opportunity. In an unequal fight, two against one, they beat up the fake prince and rob him.

Startled by the noise, hotel guests notify the police, who arrive at the Grand Bay late at night. By this time, however, Anthony has long since run away; he has no desire to have to deal with the authorities again. Following the formalities, one of the officials contacts the Saudi embassy and informs them about the attack on one of their noble members. This is the moment when the pillars of Anthony's illusory world begin to crack. The embassy claims never to have heard of "Khalid bin Al Saud." One of the detectives comments on the surprising turn of events as follows: "I have arrested many impostors in my life. But one impersonating a prince? That's pretty brazen."

The manhunt for the fugitive is successful after only a short time. Anthony Gignac is located in Chicago and brought back to Florida, where he has to answer for several counts of imposture. While he waits in jail for the trial to begin, he pulls off another coup. He contacts a lawyer named Oscar Rodriguez by phone and poses to him as Prince Khalid bin Al Saud. Anthony promises Rodriguez that he will become the family's lawyer if he helps him escape prison. The man can't possibly pass up this opportunity and agrees. So it happens that in August 1994, the lawyer pays bail in the amount of 46,000 dollars and thus gives Anthony his freedom. However, he cannot move so completely freely because two bail agents follow him at every turn until his alleged father pays the necessary money to lift the guard.

However, when the payment fails to materialize, Anthony instructs his companions to take him to the offices of American Express in Miami. Thanks to accomplices within the company, he manages to leave the building with a "black card," or black credit card, with a limit of $200 million. This convinces the bail bondsmen and the lawyer that Prince Al Saud must indeed be genuine.

Anthony embarks on a month-long shopping spree with his new acquisition in his pocket. His shopping list includes expensive watches, food, and clothing worth several thousand dollars. But his appearance does not make an impression on everyone. The assistant manager of a Ralph Lauren store describes her encounter with Anthony as follows:

"He was very entitled and kept saying, 'I want that. Bring it to me now!' He told everyone he was a prince and filthy rich, so he took himself very seriously." He allegedly wore size 34 clothes, but that was not true. She said she had him try on a size 38 piece, and it fit like a glove.

Anthony also uses his credit card to indulge in shenanigans. For example, he flies to Michigan for the day, then travels back in the evening, booking every first-class seat in his name. In this way, he guarantees to sit there alone; after all, a prince cannot fly with the "lower people."

However, American Express soon notices that something can't be right with "Khalid bin Al Saud" and contacts the authorities. Anthony is in New York at the time, where he claims an entire floor of the Four Seasons luxury hotel for himself. Unsuspecting, he enjoys a glass of champagne and the breathtaking view of the Empire State Building, the Statue of Liberty, and the Twin Towers, until one afternoon, the lawyer Oscar Rodriguez and the two bail bondsmen suddenly appear on the scene. Anthony threatens the men by contacting the Saudi embassy and refuses to comply with their request to accompany him to Florida.

"If you don't come ..." one of the agents retorts, " ... we'll throw you out the fucking window."

The threat eventually convinces the fake prince to fly with them to Miami. Once at the New York airport, he makes a desperate attempt to escape his pending prison sentence. At the top of his lungs, he yells across the terminal that he is Prince Khalid bin Al Saud and that the three men are trying to kidnap him. One of them even has a gun on him, he says.

Within seconds, Rodriguez and the two bail bondsmen are surrounded by police officers, staring fixedly into half a dozen shotgun barrels. However, the men are not so quick to admit defeat and hold an official document under the officers' noses. The document states that Al Saud is a criminal and that they will accompany him - the policemen then let them go. To prevent something like this from happening to them again on the way back, Anthony's companions rent a car and drive the 24 hours or so back to Miami on their own - they stow the fake prince in the trunk.

Anthony then spends six years in prison before being released in the early 2000s. Due to a botched escape, he landed himself a seven-month solitary confinement during his stay. He set fire to his cell, hoping that the guards would slip on the shampoo he spread on the floor. The responsible officials found this anything but amusing.

There is no trace of rehabilitation in the boy, who has now grown into a man with a roundish face, small nose, and pot-cut hairstyle. He continued to commit credit card fraud and was promptly arrested again in January 2003. Meanwhile, his existence as an impostor has taken on such proportions that he seems to believe his tall tales. For him, Prince Khalid is not just a name and, at the same time, the key to a lavish life - in his eyes, he is Prince Khalid bin Al Saud, son of the King of Saudi Arabia, and deserves to be treated accordingly. This assumption is supported by an expert opinion in which experts attest Anthony has a combined personality disorder.

The fake prince will not be released until 2013. But his time in prison has not brought him closer to honesty and insight into his faulty behavior. On the contrary, he wants to bring out the big guns to put his plan for power into action. To start his plan, Anthony makes the acquaintance of underwater photographer Annette Robertson and her husband, the famous painter Wyland. The convicted fraudster tells the couple he is interested in cooperating with them to build resorts. Together, the three scout out potentially suitable properties, including the world-famous "Cheeca Lodge & Spa" in Islamordada, a Monroe County, Florida community. The fake prince is toying with the idea of purchasing the approximately 110,000-square-foot resort for a total of $200 million, but the resort's management is skeptical. They don't trust Anthony's story about his alleged origins and make inquiries to play it safe. They come across the alleged prince's extensive criminal record and notify the authorities, whereupon Anthony is sent to prison for another year for attempted fraud.

Meanwhile, the couple reproaches themselves for not having seen through their new acquaintance's fairy tale sooner since there were countless clues. For example, when Annette brought one of Anthony's acquired pictures of her husband to the "nobleman's" home. She noticed that in the entire building, which the prince said belonged to his brother, there was not one unusual painting hanging on the wall. A Saudi Arabian prince would not decorate his house with ordinary hardware store decorations. In addition, Annette wonders in retrospect about Anthony's frequent physical contact. He hugged her in greeting and shook Wyland's hand - also strange behavior from a man who pretends to be a mannerly sheik.

When the fake prince is released from prison for the eleventh time, he immediately continues to work on the implementation of his plan: through a British asset manager named Carl Martin Williamson, who lives in North Carolina, he founds an investment firm for the super-rich. Anthony makes the cooperation public on July 26, 2015, on the LinkedIn platform with the following words:

"It is my pleasure to announce that my friend and business partner Carl M. Williamson has started a new company that will bring together people from different companies. Mr. Williamson is an honest and loyal man with excellent people skills. His company 'Martin Williamson International' will help people protect their assets from the dangers of the business world and develop new business ideas on behalf of his clients."

The business model is described as full-bodied with high profits, which are to be made possible, among other things, by "Aramco." All one has to do is acquire shares in this Saudi oil production company via Martin Williamson International. Anthony attracts 26 investors with this scam and can scam eight million dollars in one year, of which five million even come from Switzerland.

With the money, Anthony is now fulfilling more dreams and lives out his extravagant lifestyle with private jets, yachts, his own apartments, and bodyguards to the fullest. However, one thing still keeps him going: the acquisition of his own resort, or at least part of it. This time he has his eye on the legendary "Fontainebleau Miami Beach." In the past, you could meet celebrities like Elvis Presley at the bar here; today, it is struggling with impending insolvency. For "Khalid bin Al Saud," this was the ideal opportunity to kill two birds with one stone.

And so, on March 24, 2017, he contacts the billionaire and simultaneous owner of the "Fontainebleau," Jeffery Soffer, with an offer to purchase part of the hotel for a whopping 440 million dollars. In addition, the fake prince invites him to his home to discuss further details of the potential deal.

Soffer jumps at the offer, and a short time later, his finger presses the doorbell to Prince Khalid's penthouse. He appears on the doorstep and gives the billionaire a private tour of his property. He proudly presents his garage full of Ferraris and Rolls Royces, all of which have diplomatic license plates. According to "Khalid," these allow him to speed through Miami without consequence.

Although a final deal does not materialize for the time being after the meeting, the men intend to continue their negotiations. Anthony, however, still has an idea of how he can profit from Soffer in the meantime. He claims that in his country, it is customary to present the prince with generous gifts during a contract negotiation in order to win his favor. Without questioning this, the businessman then allows Anthony to take flights in his private jet and gives him jewelry worth more than $50,000. One of these trips finally takes the men to the Aspen,

Colorado ski resort, where they want to wrap up the purchase between the breathtaking backdrop of the snow-covered Rocky Mountains. In the process, however, the fake prince makes a momentous mistake when he orders prosciutto during dinner - an Italian ham made from pork and actually forbidden to devout Muslims.

Back in Florida, Soffer immediately sets a private security firm on Anthony to spy on him. He wants to be sure about the true identity of his business partner because one thing is certain: he is by no means a Saudi prince. The investigations eventually uncover Khalid bin Al Saud's real name, Anthony Gignac. Soffer summarizes the collected information in a report and hands it over to the Federal Bureau of Investigation (FBI).

When the officers search Anthony's penthouse shortly afterward, they discover that his countless Rolex watches, rings, and bracelets are, in fact, cheap copies. The means of transportation are also merely leased; the car license plates are purchased for $79 on eBay.

On November 19, 2017, Anthony Gignac was caught at JFK Airport in New York. As he is led out of the building in handcuffs, he asks, "Why don't you arrest Carl too?" Anthony is referring to the British asset manager at whose hands he scammed tens of millions of dollars.

About a month later, in the early morning of December 14, 2017, Williamson stands in the kitchen with one of his sons preparing breakfast. Suddenly, dozens of police officers storm into his home with guns drawn and interrogate the British wealth manager for six hours while his home office is turned inside out. After the FBI leaves the family home without any evidence of Williamson's knowing involvement in Gignac's scams, the latter affirms to his wife that he did not know the alleged prince was, in fact, an impostor. Around 7:30 p.m., he skips dinner because he is tired and wants to go to bed early. Carl closes the bedroom door behind him and scribbles a short note in which he asks his family for forgiveness. He then hangs himself.

In May 2019, Anthony Gignac pleads guilty. The now 47-year-old man is then sentenced to 18 years in prison for fraud, identity theft, and pretending to be a foreign diplomat.

"All the blame lies with me, and I accept that. But I am not a monster," the impostor comments on the sentence.

This time, the prison stay also heralds the end of his former life. All that remains of his luxury is the memory and his Instagram account with the numerous pictures and videos on which he stages himself and his illusory world - an Instagram account that, like "Khalid bin Al Saud" and his innocent business partner Carl Williamson, is dead.

*THE GREATEST HONOR YOU CAN DO TO
A PERSON IS TO HAVE CONFIDENCE IN
THEM.*

- *Matthias Claudius* (1740-1815),
German poet and journalist -

CHAPTER 8

GIRL, YOU KNOW IT'S TRUE

A flurry of flashlights lights up the room as the two men stride onto the stage one after the other. Reporters crowd the front row as their cameras click nonstop.

"Line up! Line up, boys!"

The men comply with the instructions, wrapping their arms around each other and turning left and right in subtle peace signs, mouths clenched into smiles. After a while, and dozens of pictures in all poses for the photographers later, they settle down on two chairs at a long table with a white tablecloth. Each of them has a cable microphone on a small tripod in front of them, which they casually adjust a bit.

"I think you should know the two gentlemen to my left!" says a blond-haired man who has taken a seat next to the two. But the reporters present are not satisfied with that. They want the young men to introduce themselves.

"My name is Fabrice Morvan," one of the two finally says after some bustling. A bandana with a golden pattern holds up his black, waist-length dreadlocks. He has paired it with a dark suit and turtleneck sweater.

"Uh ... m ... my name is Robert Pilate," his seatmate stammers in broken English with a laugh in his voice. He also has long black hair sticking out from under a bandana;

sideburns are visible on his cheeks. He wears a gray T-shirt with a print over it and a jacket studded with gold studs.

Morvan and Pilatus are also known to the masses as the band called "Milli Vanilli" - one of the world's most famous singing duos from Germany in the late 1980s. But the career of the two, which began so successfully, ends abruptly in the early 90s with a scandal. They were accused of not singing the songs themselves on the million-selling recordings. Their part allegedly consisted merely of moving their lips in sync with the songs sung by other musicians. An accusation that Morvan and Pilate deny. So vehemently that on November 19, 1990, they hold a press conference at Ocean Way Recording Studios, Hollywood, to convince the public of their innocence.

The later "Milli Vanilli" band members met in a dance school in 1988. Robert "Rob" Pilatus was born in Munich on June 8, 1964, the son of a US soldier and a German stripper. At the age of three, a Munich family adopts him. It is not known why the boy does not grow up with his biological parents.

His singing partner, Fabrice "Fab" Morvan, was born in Paris on May 14, 1966, and moved to Germany at the age of 18 to work as a dance instructor.

When the two meet for the first time at the end of the 80s, no one suspects that they will one day become one of the most successful and, at the same time, most controversial German pop duos. Especially since the young men can't stand each other at first and perceive each other as a competitor; this is because Robert often faced racism, insults, and bullying during his childhood in the Bavarian capital. In the course of the 80s, however, this changes due to the hip-hop, dance, and R&B scene spilling over from the States. Suddenly, it's considered "cool" to be dark-skinned, which brings the early 20-year-old a lot of positive attention. Peers who never even paid attention to him before now want to spend time with him, and he is also the center of attention in his dance group.

One day, however, the image of a tall, handsome man is reflected in the mirrors of the rehearsal room. He answers to the name Fabrice, who comes from France, and shares one thing in common with Robert: his skin color. From now on, Robert is no longer the only one who can enjoy his place at the center of the dance group, which goes against his grain. Fabrice is not unaware of the displeasure of his colleague, whom he perceives as arrogant and rather full of himself. He, therefore, jokingly calls him "Star."

For months, the two give each other the cold shoulder until one of them finally makes a move. The young men start talking. They discover that they have more in common than they thought, especially in the area of xenophobia.

The initial adversaries soon develop into a close-knit team. Robert and Fabrice become close friends, even move into an apartment together and support each other on their journey through life. Because the two also have one thing in common: their irrepressible will to become famous with music, to stand on stage and feel the waves of the audience's thunderous applause on their sweaty skin. In any case, they already have the prerequisites for this. Everywhere they appear together, the young women fall at their feet and are overwhelmed by the incredible charisma and beauty of the duo. And so it happens that through their nightly excursions in Munich's nightlife, they find their way to the "P1"; at that time, one of the hottest nightclubs in Munich. There they make contact with the music producer Ralph Siegel, and through him, they get the opportunity to make music together under the name "Empire Bizarre." Shortly after, their first single, "Dansez," is released, which is characterized by its synthesizer sounds. However, the hoped-for commercial success fails to materialize.

A live performance of the song on a local Bavarian radio station provides the possible reason. The show performance of the duo stands out with a coherent dance performance, but what is missing is a trademark. Something that sets Rob and Fab apart from the rest of the music on offer in show business. Funky outfits are not everything - the whole package has to be right. At the moment, the two are presenting themselves with a mixture of hip-hop, R&B, and pop and don't quite seem to know where they want to go.

But the fact that they have potential has not gone unnoticed in the music scene because the Saarland music producer Frank Farian becomes aware of Rob and Fab. After his worldwide mega-success with the disco formation "Boney M!", the blond-haired man with the radiant white smile is looking for something new - and already has an idea: In a Frankfurt club, he once heard an underground single called "Girl you know it's true," sung by "Nunmarx," a band from the American city of Baltimore. The song has a striking baseline and is catchy, but the band is completely unknown. So Farian secured the rights to the single, produced it completely from scratch, and had his American singer friend Brad Howell sing the lyrics.

Thanks to his outstanding soul voice, the no-name song became a hit in no time. But that's not enough for Farian. He wants to take the project to the next level, sell records, produce music videos, and storm the charts. What the song doesn't have yet, however, is a suitable interpreter. He would hardly be considered for it, and the actual singer Brad Howell doesn't fit either. Maybe as a new hit for his project "Boney M! No, he is no longer in the mood for that. Something completely new is needed. Something that will make the teenie-boppers boil, á la

Modern Talking. So the right faces had to be found, and Farian thought he had found them in the duo "Empire Bizarre."

Sometime later, Fabrice and Robert are standing in the Saarland music producer's studio. They are just looking for new jobs as background dancers, but Farian then reveals his new project to them. The two are immediately taken with the idea and try a few show acts. At that moment, a smile spreads across the music producer's face. A hit! Fab and Rob fit like a glove.

All the duo needs now is a suitable name. The three think back and forth for a long time and come to no coherent result, then suddenly Farian's right hand and, at the same time, ex-wife Ingrid Segieth enters the studio - nickname "Milli." And that's when it clicks. Fab and Rob add another "Vanilli" to the end, sign a contract with Sony BMG, and call themselves "Milli Vanilli" from then on.

But is it really enough for them to act as lip-syncers and dancers when they actually dreamed of making music themselves? Rob and Fab don't waste a thought on it at that time. After all, it's not even clear whether "Milli Vanilli" will be well received by the public. Moreover, they are aware that producer Frank Farian has already made a name for himself in the music scene and that it is, therefore, a great opportunity for them to be able to work with the man. If their voices aren't used on this song, they'll be used on the next one.

Until then, however, there is still a long way to go. Although the first song and the concept behind the band are now in place, the whole thing must somehow be transported to the outside world. The right marketing strategy is crucial here. Photo shoots, video shoots, TV appearances, and professional styling - in the weeks that follow, Rob and Fab go through everything that comes with show business. And it pays off. When the song hits the record stores a short time later, it immediately jumps to No. 1 in the singles charts and can't be ousted from there for weeks. Soon the success spills over to Spain, Italy, the Netherlands, and England until it finally finds its way to America.

From then on, things went steadily uphill for Rob and Fab. Due to their extraordinary style and their impressive charisma, they are regular guests on radio shows and TV shows, their faces smile at the raving teenagers from the front page and enclosed posters in magazines. "Milli Vanilli" have become international megastars virtually overnight.

Part of Farian's successful marketing strategy is to get the duo to move to London. In his opinion, only those who also have a number 1 single in England are destined for worldwide success. But since the song initially flops there, the producer sends his protégés to Ibiza because he knows that English vacationers frequent the island. All the discotheques along the party mile in San Antonio are then supplied with records, and the two main characters are invited to the respective parties. The move immediately has the desired effect. The English vacationers like the song so much that they run to the stores at home and buy the record.

However, life in the limelight also has its downsides. As much as Rob and Fab enjoy the constant festivities and attention, the music business is also tough, and they don't know how to deal with it. On a whim, they give away expensive watches and occasionally fall into cocaine consumption. Their environment observes that the two are increasingly growing into their roles. For example, if they were still reserved at their first photo shoot, they suddenly want to have their say at the second photo session and think they know everything better.

"It's very, very hard to process success," Ingrid Segieth cautions, "and I think it's even harder to process success when you haven't actually contributed that much to it; when you're just a puppet."

Although they pretend to be performers to the outside world, Rob and Fab also merely mimic lip movements on the following released songs. The curious thing is that at that time, no one seems to notice that while the vocals come across in flawless English, the alleged singers struggle to manage a proper sentence in that language in interviews. Especially Rob has a strong Bavarian accent.

The dream of having their own single is not fulfilled for the two. Although they take singing lessons and warble along on the playback recordings of the sequels, they continue to act merely as performers in the music videos and at appearances. To make the performances as convincing as possible, Rob and Fab soon believe they are their own voices. The desire for self-realization remains unbroken.

Over time, the duo's notoriety seems to make Robert's megalomania grow immeasurably. Among other things, this leads to him preferring to watch a boxing match with Mike Tyson instead of playing in front of thousands of spectators at a scheduled gig on the same evening. Another time, he gets up in the middle of a live interview with a Canadian television station. He leaves the room, whereupon the baffled host is forced to interview Fabrice alone. To American newspapers, he loudly proclaims that "Milli Vanilli" is more musically talented than any Bob Dylan, Paul McCartney, or Mick Jagger. "I'm the new modern rock 'n' roll. I'm the new Elvis."

For the next big step in their career, the duo is aiming for a tour of America. But both Farian and they are strictly against it - the worry is too great that one of the playback devices could go on strike and thus bring down the entire construct of lies. Rob and Fab override the objections and tour the USA anyway.

The inevitable happens. On July 21, 1989, the record company's fears become reality. Rob and Fab play a concert in Bristol, Connecticut, broadcast live on MTV's music channel. During the performance of their hit "Girl, you know it's true," everything goes according to plan at first. The duo performs and encourages the cheering audience to sing along. Once again, they feel like megastars. During the chorus, however, the playback tape suddenly gets stuck. It sounds like a broken record, where one part is repeated over and over again.

"Girl, you know it's ...krchz... Girl you know it's ...krchz... Girl you know it's ..."

Rob first tries to cover the breakdown, but shortly afterward, he leaves the stage in a hurry. Fab runs after him and tries behind the scenes to persuade his partner to come back out on stage. Impossibly, they can stop the concert already after the second song. Since the problem with the tape has been solved in the meantime, Rob lets himself be persuaded and trots back to the audience like a beaten dog. Strangely enough, no one there noticed anything about the mishap. Everyone assumes that the hang-up is part of the show or a kind of remix, which is why they welcome the duo back with thunderous applause.

The situation is anything but fun for the record company and everyone involved in the tour. True to the motto "We told you so," the tour manager writes an angry fax to Robert Pilate:

"You are on the best way to destroy YOUR career. You are not allowed to play from now on, today no more:

    a.) sing "We want pussy - we want pussy" acapella
    b.) dance and move as if you two are fucking each other
    c.) flee from the stage if something doesn't work technically
    d.) act politically provocatively. You are not allowed to hit on the most beautiful white girl on stage in areas that are white and tease her.

You are not prima donnas. Even faster than you went up, you're going to fall down. You will be kicked into the ground; the media is just waiting for it. Therefore, there are only two possibilities:

    a.) you change your behavior immediately
    b.) you stop the tour, and we train for three months until you can behave like superstars."

The heated atmosphere reaches its boiling point when Rob and Fab are awarded the most important American music prize on February 21, 1990.

"And the Grammy in the category of 'best new artist' goes to ..." says the laudator, opening the envelope in his hand, "... "Milli Vanilli"!"

A deafening shriek and thunderous applause instantly echo through the Shrine Auditorium in Los Angeles. Rob and Fab are beaming in each other's arms and come rushing onto the stage shortly after, waving after being handed the golden gramophone, the two-step in front of the microphone.

"We would like to say thank you very much ..." Robert announces, " ... and we would like to point out that there are a lot of talented artists here tonight, there are a lot of artists out there who can achieve the same as we did today. This award is for all the artists in the world, thank you very much!"

Frank Farian sinks into his chair in shame at home in front of the TV. 'Where is this going?" he thinks to himself.

Only a short time after their rocket-like rise, "Milli Vanilli" has achieved what other musicians can only dream of. They are among the stars of their time, lead a life of luxury, and were recently awarded a Grammy. Instead of drawing a line under their success at its peak, Rob and Fab now want to give the songs their own voice. They plan to sing themselves on the next record, come what may. But Farian refuses. Their performance is not enough to do justice to the brand. Moreover, it would then be revealed that everything was based on fraud from the very beginning. He, as a music producer, would become a worldwide laughingstock.

"It came to the scandal because we then wanted to sing, on the second album ..." says Robert in a later interview, "... and we yes then gave concerts, and sometimes the equipment failed, and we really had to sing, and people did not even realize that these are not our voices. Then we said 'Frank, we want to sing,' and he just wouldn't let us."

The dispute escalates to the point where no one can really approach the other, and no compromise can be found. Farian is therefore forced to take a radical step: He ends the collaboration with Rob and Fab, flies to New York, and holds a press conference on November 14, 1990. There he informs the world about the end of "Milli Vanilli." He does this with the words: "The boys are fired. They haven't sung a note."

Immediately, the press representatives storm out of the room and sit down at their computers. Immediately the scandal spreads like wildfire - for weeks, nothing else can be read on the front pages of the tabloids. "Milli Vanilli" CDs are publicly rolled over, the Grammy is retroactively revoked from them, and the noble-minded show business chases the two voiceless beaus to hell. Even pop titan Dieter Bohlen puts in his two cents in a newspaper interview:

"What Milli Vanilli have done is criminal. You can't deal with teen dreams like that. I was a total Beatles fan as a teenager. If someone had told me Paul McCartney wasn't singing himself, my world would have collapsed. I'm sure the Millis are exceptional in the business. There may be a few isolated cases, but the ones who are famous don't do that."

Just five days after Frank Farian's revelation, Rob and Fab give a press conference themselves on November 19, 1990, at Ocean Way Recording Studios, Hollywood, in front of over 100 curious journalists. If they initially wanted to portray Farian as a liar, the two realize quite quickly that there is no point. The press representatives present pounce on Rob and Fab like predators and force them to tell the truth.

In the end, the two stand up, grab their microphones, and hold up the golden gramophone.

"So, we're giving back the Grammy now," Rob says with an ironic smile. The deprivation of the most important music award is the final nail to "Milli Vanilli's" coffin. From this moment on, the duo is completely on their own. Nobody from their former environment supports them anymore - there is complete radio silence on the record company's part.

While Rob and Fab stay in Los Angeles, Frank Farian returns to Germany. There, Rob's adopted sister Carmen, in particular, is the scapegoat for the fans' hatred. She once accompanied her brother to his gigs, and today her mailbox often contains autograph cards of the pop duo smeared with swastikas and

"SIEG HEIL." In addition, a court decides that the aggrieved fans should all get their money back from the label for the records and concert tickets they bought. In total, around 10 million people are entitled to compensation.

The laughingstock of the nation, a faked talent, and a financial crash - with the "biggest blow of his life," Rob falls into a deep alcohol and drug addiction.

"He let himself go," Fabrice says in a later interview. "Watching him crash, oddly enough, gave me the strength to say 'no.' And not fall into the same abyss he did. He really lost it at the end. He didn't know who he was anymore, and I didn't know how to help him. We had grown up together, more or less. When we looked into each other's eyes, I knew who he was. Until a certain moment. Because now, when I looked him in the eye, I no longer recognized him. That wasn't Rob Pilate anymore."

Rob repeatedly gets into trouble with the authorities for assault and vandalism; in 1995, he is sentenced to probation for drug possession. During this time, Frank Farian stands by him financially, presumably because of remorse. He pays for Rob's lawyer and drug therapies and finances his return to Germany in 1997, where he continues to rehab in a Freiburg clinic. Farian even offers to produce a comeback record of "Milli Vanilli," but it does not come to that. On April 3, 1998, Ingrid Segieth wants to visit Rob in his hotel room in Friedrichsdorf near Frankfurt am Main. After knocking on the door for several minutes without success, she finally consults the janitor. Together they manage to gain access to Rob's room. Instantly, they freeze on the doorstep. There lies Rob's body on the floor, next to his travel bags. The subsequent autopsy reveals that he died of heart failure due to a drug and alcohol overdose. The 34-year-old's body is then buried in Munich's Waldfriedhof cemetery.

Despite the scandal, "Milli Vanilli" has left a lasting impression on pop culture. The case has sparked a major debate about authenticity and artistic integrity and contributed to a better understanding of what it means to perform a real live performance.

Fabrice has continued to make music after Rob's death and is pursuing his career as a solo artist. Among other things, he works as a DJ and producer and performs all over the world. Though a shadow lies over his career, he has continued to work hard to make his dreams come true. However, one thing has been painfully clear to him: the way down is at least as fast as the way up, especially when the world knows the truth.

*THEY MAKE THE SPIRITS APPEAR
AND ARE MUCH ADMIRED,
BUT IT IS OFTEN NOTHING BUT A LINEN
AND UNDERNEATH A BROOMSTICK.*

- Friedrich Pesendorfer (1867-1935),
Austrian theologian -

CHAPTER 9

NEWS FROM THE BEYOND

Mrs. Granger nervously rubs her palms against each other. She seems to be sitting on hot coals, sliding back and forth in her chair so restlessly. Her husband gives her a reproving look. He can well understand his wife's excitement - but she makes him nervous with her fidgeting. Besides, it's not proper for a lady to lose her composure like that. Mrs. Granger closes her eyes and takes a deep breath. "Just keep calm," she says to herself over and over again in her mind like a mantra. But it doesn't help. Infinite sadness overcomes the woman. She feels her throat tightening; tears come to her eyes. She would love to untie the ribbons of her hat, which she has tied far too tightly into a bow below her chin. The woman tries to hide her discomfort. With her head down, she smooths out her ankle-length, flared skirt before her fingers begin to pluck at the tight top with the club-shaped sleeves. Mrs. Granger is jolted out of her thoughts when the lights suddenly go out. The Granger family room is now in darkness. The lambent flame of a white candle on the cherry wood table laden with teacups, coasters, and cake plates now serves as the sole source of light. Mr. Granger feels for his wife's hand and gives her an affirming look. Then Reverend Clark takes the floor. But Mrs. Granger is so agitated that she can hardly follow the prayer of the man who is supposed to protect those present from malevolent beings. Even as the clergyman speaks his intercession, a loud knocking thunders through the room. Mrs. Granger lets out a gasp of shock, which her husband acknowledges with a reprimanding look. "It seems to be working!" she thinks. The initial shock immediately gives way to relief. Hopefully, Mrs. Granger smiles at her little daughter Kate and the medium Maggie. Leah, Maggie's older sister, gives Mrs. Granger a thoughtful look - as if it were sacrilegious to even doubt the medium's abilities. Knock, knock, knock, knock sounds again. "It's the murdered peddler. He's asking for the alphabet," Leah whispers. "Did God send you?" asks Reverend Clark, who had been jolted out of his prayer by the unexpected knocks. No sooner has the clergyman uttered the question than two short knocks sound again. They mean "yes."

The man frowns, puts the thumb and forefinger of his right hand to his chin, and ponders aloud, "But what can God's purpose be in this? Is His plan so important that He must use such a manifestation from the spirit world for its fulfillment?" KNOCK, KNOCK - stronger and more insistent than before. Those present, gathered around the table, cringe as the cherry wood table suddenly begins to bounce up and down as if by magic. The clinking of teacups on their coasters shatters the spellbound silence in the room. As the table quiets again, Maggie announces in a whisper, "The ghost of Harriet Granger has appeared!" Now Mrs. Granger can no longer hold back her tears. She buries her face in her hands and begins to sob. "My beloved child ... we ... we miss you ... so much," are the only words she can produce in a choked voice. Even Mr. Granger can no longer hide his feelings now. In the candlelight, some believe they can see water sparkling in the eyes of the visibly moved man. Since the death of their daughter, the grieving parents have been plagued by a pressing question: was daughter Harriet murdered by her husband? Two knocking sounds ring out, confirming the grieving couple's assumption. But the ghost of Harriet has another troubling message for the Grangers. As one of the attendants recites the alphabet and the spirit of Harriet signifies with a short knock which letters to write down, a phrase forms, "Beware, now he seeks your life!" Eyes widening in fear, Mrs. Granger stares into her husband's shocked face. "Don't be afraid. Now that we know about the danger, we can take precautions," the man tries to reassure his wife and himself. At the end of the seance, Reverend Clark presses one more question. "Harriet, what is it like in heaven?" he inquires and begins to recite the alphabet. Knock. He notes the letter and starts over. So it goes on until the man's note reads, "More wonderful than you can imagine."

In the small town of Hydesville in the American state of New York, the couple John and Margaret Fox have lived with their two youngest daughters in a rented wooden cottage since the beginning of 1848. The simple dwelling stands on a plot of tall grass and is surrounded by tall trees and spreading shrubs.

The family leads a simple and unremarkable life. But just three months after they moved into the wooden cottage, that changes abruptly. One night, it is March of 1848, the couple is roused from sleep by the anguished cry of their 14-year-old daughter, Margaretta. "Mother!" it echoes over to them. John and Margaret jump out of bed and rush to their daughters, who are sleeping together in a room under the roof. As Mr. and Mrs. Fox pull open the door to the bedroom, they see Margaretta, called "Maggie," and her sister Catherine - Kate - sitting excitedly in their beds. The girls look at their parents with wide eyes. "What happened?" their mother asks. "We heard strange noises, really scary!" explains Maggie. John and Margaret look at the girls in perplexity - they had not been able to hear any unusual sounds in their bedchamber.

But before the couple can reassure Maggie and Kate, the silence is broken by three knocks in succession. It sounds like someone is pounding on the wall of the room. "What is it?" cries Maggie, almost hysterically. The eerie knocking sounds again while the couple searches for a rational explanation.

John listens spellbound into the silence that follows. He, too, feels his heart now hammering firmly against his ribcage. But he hears only the wind whistling around the house and rattling the shutters. "Maybe it's just a branch hitting the facade," he tries to reassure himself, knowing full well that the sound didn't sound like that at all.

"Take your pillows and quilts. You're sleeping with us tonight," Margaret decides without further ado. The girls gather up their sleeping things and creep fearfully behind their parents down the hall to their bedroom. They snuggle close together and listen tensely to the silence, but they are not startled again by the eerie tapping noises on that moonless night. Only the wind continues to whistle around the wooden cottage, and thick raindrops patter against the windows. Fatigue soon defeats excitement, and one family member after another sinks into a fitful sleep.

The next night, as usual, Maggie and Kate go to their sleeping chamber under the roof. But no sooner have the girls made themselves comfortable in their beds than they startle up again. KNOCK, KNOCK, KNOCK. This time the sound seems louder and more insistent than the night before. It takes only a few seconds before the parents are standing in their daughters' room again - this time, they have heard the terrifying thumping in the house.

But unlike last night, the knocking noises don't want to stop. Hour after hour passes. KNOCK, KNOCK, KNOCK, KNOCK, it echoes from the wooden walls. Sleep is now out of the question. The more often the sounds resound, the more anxious the family members become. Even the mother, Margret, soon can no longer hide her fear of her almost hysterical daughters. Only the father, John, tries not to let on how uneasy he feels. The night passes over the estate - without any of the family members getting a wink of sleep.

All four remain wide awake during the nights to come. Only sometimes can exhaustion overcome the fear in one or the other, forcing them into a dreamless sleep. Meanwhile, the knocking noises seem to get louder and louder from night to night. KNOCK! KNOCK! KNOCK! KNOCK! Even their beds, the table, and the chairs in the children's room seem to tremble.

It is a moonless, silent night when suddenly another pounding is heard, this time at the house's front door. John bravely rushes toward the noise and pulls open the front door. But he only looks into the darkness. There is no one there. Margret seems close to a nervous breakdown from fear and lack of sleep. And Maggie and Kate are also stricken. John doesn't know what to do. "I'm sure it's just some neighborhood youths trying to scare us," he tries to reassure his family, but mostly himself.

The next morning, the eldest son of the family visits his parents. Margret confides in him. "I think this house is haunted," she finishes describing the previous nights. "Oh, Mother," David replies, "that's nonsense. I'm very sure there's a simple and logical explanation." Before David leaves his parents' house again, he asks his mother, "Please do me a favor and don't tell your scary story to the neighbors." The young man fears that his family will be ridiculed in town and thought to be feeble-minded. His mother only acknowledges her son's request with a contemptuous sigh.

As the day draws to a close and dusk sets in, the knocking sounds that cannot be ignored resound once again. The Fox couple searches the entire house to get to the bottom of the cause of these eerie sounds. Meanwhile, Maggie and Kate sit shivering on one of their beds, clinging to each other fearfully.

After John and Margret have unsuccessfully combed every nook and cranny of the cottage, they are no closer to finding the cause of the noises, but they have come to a realization. The knocking is loudest in their daughters' room. The father positions himself in front of the room door; the mother positions herself in the girls' room. There it sounds again: KNOCK! KNOCK! KNOCK! KNOCK! "The sound seems to be coming from around the walls where the door is embedded," John muses with a furrowed brow. But who or what is causing the knocking and what to do about it, the family man doesn't know. He finds it strange that the knocking sounds only occur when one of his daughters is nearby. The strange sounds only stop when the girls have fallen asleep. Margret is certain, "The ghost is depending on the presence of Maggie and Kate to be able to knock." This is a troubling thought for the parents. "It seems like someone is trying to come out of the wall," Maggie tells her mother in a voice filled with fear.

It's not just the intensity of the knocking sounds that increase from night to night. One night, the mother is startled by her daughters' shrill cries and runs to the girls' room - as she had done so many times in the previous days. "What happened?" asks Margret, quite out of breath. Maggie and Kate, who by now prefer to share a bed rather than fall asleep alone, report that they felt something heavy settle on their feet. It was as if a dog had jumped into their bed and made itself comfortable at the end of the bed. Except the family doesn't own a pet. Another time, Kate claims to have felt an ice-cold hand on her face. Pieces of furniture are no longer in their original places in the sisters' room at dawn, and at night, the girls report, something keeps pulling the covers off their beds. For weeks now, the eerie noises have robbed the family of sleep. Especially Margret, but also John, slowly believe they're losing their minds.

On March 31, 1848, Margret insists that the family go to bed early. The woman feels physically exhausted and believes the flu is coming on. As dusk falls, all family members gather in the parental bedroom - for safety reasons, as the mother explains.

No sooner have the four of them snuggled into bed: knock, knock, knock. "It's starting again!" cries Maggie, bursting into tears in despair. Margret takes her daughter in her arms and tries to comfort her. KNOCK! KNOCK! KNOCK! The sound increases in intensity as the family becomes more anxious. "I know what it could be," Kate suddenly says into the tense silence, "maybe someone is playing an April Fool's joke on us. Tomorrow is April 1, after all!" But the mother no longer believes it's a joke. And if it should be one, it doesn't meet her sense of humor.

Suddenly, the 11-year-old girl jumps out of bed. "I have an idea! We could try talking to the ghost! Maybe he'll answer us!" Kate fearlessly explains her plan. Before anyone can voice their concerns, the girl shouts, "Mr. Splitfoot! Do it after me!" then the little girl claps her hands twice. Margret winces at the word " split foot" - because that's how the devil is referred to in her area.

After a short silence: knock, knock. Kate opens her eyes in disbelief and makes an astonished sound. Her 14-year-old sister is infected by the younger girl's thirst for adventure. She also jumps out of the master bed and stands next to Kate. "Now follow my lead!" shouts Maggie, clapping her hands firmly four times. The answer comes immediately: knock, knock, knock. Excitedly, she jiggles her little sister's arm, "Did you hear that? It's working; Mr. Splitfoot is really answering us!" John and Margret sit up in bed, paralyzed with fear. The mother claws at the soft upper bed. The father of the family cannot share his daughters' joy either.

The fear of the previous nights seems to have evaporated in the girls. Giggling, Kate holds two fingers in the air. Knock! Knock! Chuckling, the 11-year-old turns to her mother, "Look, Mr. Splitfoot not only hears well, but he also sees excellently!" Curiosity slowly gets the better of the family mother, too. "Maybe it really is a ghost haunting our house and trying to communicate with us? Maybe our house is a portal to the world of the dead," the wife whispers into the silence of the room while her husband rolls his eyes, slowly wondering if Margret has lost her mind.

"You try it, too. Ask him a question," Maggie encourages her mother. Margret clears her throat before calling into the dark room in a quivering voice, "Tell me, how many children do I have?" After a brief pause, the noises begin. The mother begins to count: knock, knock, knock, knock, knock. Six. "I guess your Mr. Splitfoot got it wrong," Margret comments on the knocked answer, seemingly relieved that whoever made a mistake.

"No," Maggie replies, "it's right." She reminds her mother of a child who died only a short time after birth.

The mother now wants to know exactly, "Are you a person who will answer my questions?" This time it remains silent. "Are you a spirit? Then I challenge you to knock twice!" Margret resolutely drills on. No sooner has she uttered her question: KNOCK, KNOCK, so loud that the bed shakes. "Have you been hurt in this house?" continues Maggie. KNOCK,

KNOCK. So the game goes back and forth for quite a while until the family learns that it is the ghost of a man. The then 34-year-old was killed in the house before the killer buried his body ten feet deep in the basement. The dead man left behind his wife, three daughters, and two sons. Only a short time after the brutal murder, his wife died, and his children were orphans from then on.

"Phew," sighs Margret, "you've been through some bad things. If I go get our neighbors so they can meet you, would you talk to them, too?" Knock, knock. Reluctantly, John crawls out of the warm bed at his wife's behest, pulls on his robe, and steps out into the cold evening air. Quickly he makes his way to Mrs. Redfield's house. The neighbor raises an eyebrow in disbelief when she hears why Mr. Fox wants her to come to his house. "Surely the girls are just playing a trick on their parents," the woman thinks as she slips on her coat and slips into her shoes.

Mrs. Redfield quickly dismisses her suspicions, however, when she sees the Fox girls, now quite pale and frightened, sitting on the bed with Margret and clinging tightly to their mother's arms - apparently, the thought of communicating with a dead person in the afterlife had made him queasy after all. Only a few seconds later, the neighbor also hears the frightening noises. Knock, knock, knock; short pause; KNOCK! KNOCK! KNOCK! "But that's impossible!" exclaims Mrs. Redfield, visibly frightened. "It's just as I told you," John replies in a matter-of-fact voice, "it's been going on for weeks, always at night. We've searched every corner of the house. There's nothing here that can cause the knocking sounds."

"I'll get my husband," Mrs. Redfield says and hurries off. Like wildfire, word spreads through the small town that the Fox family home is haunted. Soon, about 15 neighbors have gathered in the cramped wooden cottage. Stunned but also excited, they listen to the acoustic signals of the ghost, which he gives them in response to the questions asked.

Soon those present have found out more information about the dead man because gradually, it is possible for the dead man's soul to answer more complex questions, in which one of the living present recites the alphabet, and the spirit knocks at the necessary letter. In this way, whole sentences are then formed peu à peu. "Charles B. Rosna," as he was known, had been a peddler during his lifetime. On a Tuesday evening 5 years ago, his life had been brutally taken from him in one of the bedrooms in the current Fox house. His attacker maltreated him with a butcher knife until he no longer made a sound. The motive of the murderer was greed. He had stolen 500 dollars from him - converted and adjusted for inflation, the amount today corresponds to a value of around 20,000 USD. The ghost also knew the name of his murderer: John Bell.

After none of those present can think of a meaningful question, one of the neighbors says: "John, you and the children - you shouldn't sleep here tonight. I have plenty of room in the house; you're welcome to stay at my place." Margret thinks it's a good idea, and the two girls also seem happy not to have to sleep in the haunted house for a night. Only John waves it off. He wants to stay home and keep watch in case there are any unexplained phenomena again. Mr. Redfield agrees to spend the night in the haunted house with his neighbor. But when morning comes, no more eerie incidents had occurred.

Soon all the residents of Hydesville know about the mysterious happenings at the Fox house. Margret is annoyed that she did not listen to her son David's advice not to tell the neighbors about the strange knocking noises.

Almost all the inhabitants of the town make a pilgrimage to the inconspicuous wooden cottage with the overgrown garden and knock on the front door. They, too, want to talk to the spirit and get rid of their most pressing questions. "Is there life after death?", "What will my life be like in the future?", "How are my deceased loved ones?", "Will I reap a bountiful harvest this year?" - are just some of the questions that the spirit answers to the townspeople at dusk, knocking.

"It's almost like a siege," scolds John, visibly annoyed by the constant visit. But the guests never tire of eliciting all kinds of secrets from the ghost. When a neighbor asks whether the knocking is a gift from God, the sound is: knock, knock. Up to 300 people stand around the Fox family estate, waiting for an opportunity to communicate with the spirit. The being from the other world comforts the residents of Hydesville by assuring them that there is life after death and that their relatives are well in the afterlife.

Meanwhile, the residents of Hydesville set out to find John Bell, the murderer of the peddler. While there is no record of a Charles B. Rosna once living in their town, a John Bell did exist. They track down the man in his new hometown and confront the visibly perplexed Bell with the ghost's accusations. Outraged by this accusation, the man sets out for Hydesville the same day. He wants to complain about the slanderous allegations and clear his name.

But it is no use. No one believes his testimony. However, they don't put the angry man on trial either. After all, there is only one witness, and he is a ghost. And so, John Bell returns home, upset but a free man.

The weeks drag on. The Fox girls' older sister, who lives in the city of Rochester in New York State, also receives reports of the events at her parents' home. The young woman sets out in May 1848 to visit her family and find out exactly what was going on in Hydesville. The young woman had become a mother at an early age. But she was still in her teens when her husband abandoned her, along with their child. Already a tough and domineering personality, she now added a ruthless severity.

Her parents have meanwhile holed up with Maggie and Kate in the house of brother David. The crowd of onlookers has become too great at the Fox house, with its resident from beyond the grave. Although Margret literally begs the ghost to leave her and her family alone, the being does not comply with her request. Slowly, the onlookers are joined by visitors who obviously express their skepticism about the haunting. In silence, John thanks God that the time when women believed to be witches were burned at the stake is long gone. Otherwise, the man is sure his wife and daughters would have been burning in flames long ago. His assumption is confirmed by some clergymen who offer the father of the family to perform an exorcism on the Fox women.

The ghostly creature now begins to make mischief in David's house and terrorizes its inhabitants at night with terrifying knocking noises. The something from beyond seems to be not bound to a place but to a person.

Leah decides to take her little sister Kate with her on her return trip to Rochester. Perhaps, the young woman hopes, the portal to the afterlife will close when the girls are separated. But to everyone's horror, just the opposite occurs. The spirit seems to have more abilities than the family had previously believed. The being is able to be in several places at once. While Leah is still on her way home with her little sister, the mysterious knocking noises begin and continue when they arrive in Rochester. It becomes more and more apparent: the ghost seems to be holding onto the two youngest Fox girls.

One night, Leah lies in her bed, unable to find sleep. Her thoughts circle: one idea follows another. The idea that there must be more to her sisters' talent keeps her awake. Then an idea comes to her. During the night, she forges a plan she wants to implement the next day. Only then is Leah overcome by fatigue. Satisfied, the young woman falls asleep.

When dawn breaks, Leah grabs a pen and paper. She writes a letter to her mother in Hydesville, suggesting to Margret that she and 14-year-old Maggie join her in Rochester. Leah would take a break from her work as a piano teacher to care for her younger sisters without restriction. The girls' potential as mediums who can make contact with the dead in the afterlife would have to be encouraged and, of course, exploited. She goes on to write to Margret that many respected Rochester residents are very interested in Maggie and Kate's talents. Among them, for example, the wealthy Granger couple, who lost their beloved daughter Harriet two years ago and would like to contact the dead girl once again. The grieving parents would have invited the Fox sisters to their home for a demonstration of their skills.

Apparently, the letter convinces Margret because only a few weeks later, she is standing on the threshold of the Granger family's living room together with Leah, Maggie, and Kate. Earlier, Leah had instructed the grieving couple. She said the room must be darkened during the séance, and the table at which the participants are seated must be made only of wood. The session opens with a protective prayer, she further explained. Questions may only be asked in such a way that the spirit can answer "yes" or "no." She said that if it wanted to tell the living more, it would knock five times in a row - that's the sign for someone to recite the alphabet. But she also warns the Granger family that if the spirit did not feel respected by those present, it would immediately retreat to the afterlife, and the opportunity to communicate with their dead daughter would be lost.

At the end of the séance, Leah is more than pleased with her sisters' performance in the Grangers' living room. The young woman immediately sets about planning Maggie and Kate's first public séance, which she has advertised throughout the city as the "Fox Sisters."

On Tuesday, November 14, 1848, the time has come; Rochester's largest venue, Corinthian Hall, hosts the first public séance of the Fox Sisters. Leah had previously drummed up publicity and had advertisements printed in the local newspaper.

A host opens the evening, first telling the paying audience about the murdered peddler with whose spirit the "Fox Sisters" can communicate and thus access other dead people in the afterlife. "This, ladies and gentlemen," the man concludes the introduction, "is not just a religion, it's a new science! You have the opportunity today to put the gift of the "Fox Sisters" to the test and see for yourselves their extraordinary talent!"

But among the audience are not only people sympathetic to the two media. To make matters worse, little Kate is also ill that evening, which is why the 14-year-old has to go on stage alone and tries desperately to ignore the disparaging comments from the audience. It was true that the sisters had often performed séances with only Leah at their side - but in a small, private setting. Never before had they performed in front of hundreds of people - and certainly not alone.

The room's lights dim. Leah grabs her little sister's hand, sweaty with excitement, and leads the youngsters onto the stage. Maggie is wearing a pale blue, flared dress with a matching tight-fitting top. She wears her dark brown hair in an updo. The color of her gown makes the girl look pale and clearly younger than 14.

Leah escorts her little sister to the wooden table on the stage, where five select members of Rochester's upper class are already seated. Encouragingly, they nod and smile at Maggie, who can barely hide her nervousness. Leah pulls out the last empty chair in the group and motions for her sister to sit down. A haunting silence fills the room until someone in the audience calls out, "Is the ghost here?" The dramatic silence is broken by a clearly audible loud knock, followed by the incredulous and fascinated murmurs of the audience.

Maggie demonstrates her gift by asking questions and waiting for the knocking answer from the ghost. Some observers from the audience are also allowed to ask questions and also receive answers from beyond the grave. After about an hour, the medium ends the seance. To the deafening applause of some audience members, Leah leads her sister off the stage. But some people in the audience still do not believe that everything is going right here and express their doubts loudly.

Two more "Fox Sisters" performances follow in the Corinthian Hall. A group of respected politicians also come on stage and convince themselves that Maggie and Kate are not tricking. None of the men can detect any deception.

For four years, Maggie and Kate remain in the ever-growing city of Rochester, holding their seances almost day and night - sometimes before large audiences, sometimes in private. Reporters from the local newspaper write praising articles and express their admiration for the "Fox Sisters."Invitations to perform in other New York cities soon followed. But the dark side of their fame soon becomes apparent to the girls. When they enter or leave the stage, some of the male guests can't help themselves and shout vulgar things at the youngsters. The foul-mouthed men believe that Maggie and Kate are the kinds of girls who would do anything for money. They also don't shy away from groping Maggie as she walks by. The now 15-year-old is quickly tired of the behavior of some guests and would like to quit. But Leah works the girls over and doesn't tolerate back talk. In 1850, she decides that her two sisters need a wider sphere of action and plans to move to New York City.

It is March of 1853 when Franklin Pierce wins the 14th presidential election of the United States and moves into the White House in the US capital, Washington, DC. His wife, First Lady Jane Appleton, cannot rejoice in her husband's political success. She lost her last son only shortly before moving to the White House. Benjamin Pierce Junior dies shortly before age 12 in a tragic train accident. Falling, heavy luggage strikes the boy to death in front of his mother. Benjamin is their third child; his siblings died in infancy and early childhood. The tragic death of her only living child plunges the First Lady into deep, unending grief. She prompts her staff to raise black flags throughout the venerable White House. While President Pierce develops a severe alcohol problem in the years following his son's death, his wife becomes aware of the fuss surrounding the "Fox Sisters." She is enthusiastic about the sisters' abilities and invites the now-famous Maggie to the White House. She asks the young woman to establish contact with her deceased Benjamin and thus enables her to communicate with her beloved child one last time. There is no lore as to what went on behind closed doors in the president's seat of government. Some believe that Jane Appleton wanted to know if Benjamin's senseless death was cosmic revenge for her husband's political ambition. What seems certain is that Maggie also sat in a room with dimmed lights at this séance and conveyed her dead son's comforting words to the First Lady from beyond the grave.

Leah and the Fox sisters strike a chord with their séances.

At the latest, after the start of the Civil War in April 1861, there is hardly a family in the country that does not mourn the loss of a beloved relative. Since time immemorial, the bereaved have yearned for comfort, for the certainty that their loved ones are no longer here but are not entirely gone. Some would even give the shirt off their back if they could express their deep affection for the deceased one last time and say "goodbye."

In addition to the many followers Maggie and Kate have, resistance is also forming against the young women's spiritualism craze. Critics accuse the Fox Sisters of promoting atheism, fanaticism, insanity, and idiocy. In the spring of 1854, two members of the US Senate submit a petition signed by no fewer than 15,000 Americans. In the petition, they demand that, among other things, the mysterious tapping noises during the sisters' seances be investigated for their origin. The question of who the members of the commission should be is causing a great deal of discussion. One politician allegedly pleaded for employees of the post office - after all, there is the possibility that there is something like a "spiritual telegraph" that connects the mortal world with the beyond.

But no matter who puts Maggie and Kate's abilities to the test, no one can explain the seemingly supernatural phenomena during the séances or even prove that the girls are cheating.

The Fox sisters' time in New York City is marked by a lot of work, little free time, and their nagging sister Leah, who pushes them to do even more. Every day, Leah makes the two teenagers slave away: She organizes three séances a day, each with 30 participants. The three women earn a total of $90 per day (equivalent to a current profit of around 2,000 USD).

Even though the money is flowing, and the "Fox Sisters" and their sister Leah are not suffering any financial hardship, they are very worried about the growing competition. Not only do their rivals put on real shows, with music played by invisible orchestras and pieces of furniture that float through the air as if by magic, but young women on stage are not stingy with their sexual charms.

Kate, in particular, tries to counter the spectacular shows of her competitors and learns, among other things, spiritual writing, in which words and entire sentences are put down on paper without the intervention of the critical ego. She also appropriates "materialization," in which the medium puts herself in a trance. She mysteriously creates matter, such as so-called "ectoplasm" - The term comes from parapsychology and is meant to describe a substance that can emerge from a medium's various orifices. Despite growing competition, most believers hold on to Maggie and Kate's spiritual abilities. The girls were too young, too uneducated, and too innocent in their early days as mediums to be able to fool highly intellectual scholars, they reason.

When the two young women are not holding a seance, they sit together in their room and drink countless glasses of wine while dreaming of handsome, charming men who will free them from the clutches of their domineering and money-grubbing sister Leah. Meanwhile, Maggie and Kate have developed a real hatred for Leah that they barely try to hide.

For Kate, the dream of freedom soon comes true. She flees to England, where she meets a spiritualist. The young couple marries and has two sons.

And for Maggie, too, a better life is in the offing in her early twenties. She meets 32-year-old US researcher, explorer, and physician Elisha Kent Kane. The young man is fascinated by the pretty medium, even though he himself is very skeptical about spiritualism. They arrange to meet and write each other touching love letters.

Leah sees Maggie's admirer as an existential threat. The man is out to destroy her family. If he marries her younger sister, then the rewarding source of income from the séances would have finally dried up for her after Kate had already sought refuge.

The couple in love marries secretly in a Quaker ceremony, according to the rites of a small Christian community, which has no legal validity. Thus, the two speak of themselves as man and wife from then on, but they escape the family disputes that would have threatened them if they had been officially married.

It is 1857 when Elisha Kent Kane suffers a severe stroke at 37 and dies as a result. Maggie falls into a deep depression because of the death of her great love. From then on, she sits alone in her darkened room, reads the letters that Kane once wrote to her, and tries to drown her sorrow in wine. She fervently wishes to give herself the same healing comfort that she had given her many clients over the years. But it doesn't work. Throughout her life, Maggie never recovers from the emotional pain that Elisha's sudden death has caused her.

Even though Maggie never marries another man, she soon regains her fighting spirit, despite her deep grief. Against the wishes of her sister Leah, the widow converts to Catholicism - she is sure that her late husband would have liked her decision.

"Time heals all wounds," the saying goes. But Maggie realizes that the wounds are simply becoming painfully scarred. When Leah insists it's time for another seance, Maggie snaps. "You're driving me crazy!" she yells at Leah, "now that you've gotten so rich off of us, you should start saving your soul from hell!".

Her younger sister's words do not touch Leah. Kate may have escaped her sphere of influence, but she won't let that happen with Maggie. She manages to wrap the grieving widow around her finger again and persuades her to conduct séance after séance over the next few years.

The year is 1888, and Maggie Fox is now in her mid-fifties. Although Kane has been dead for 31 years now, the widow still wears mourning clothes. She hasn't slept in days; she had been restlessly pacing up and down the cage of her apartment like a tiger, talking to her closest friends about her plan and draining bottle after bottle of wine. Now also widowed, Kate is also in on it and has made the trip to New York to stand by her sister.

Now, on the evening of October 21, the time has come. Maggie has summoned the public to the New York Academy of Music for an announcement. Four thousand people have answered her call. As Maggie prepares backstage for the biggest performance of her life, the audience whispers excitedly among themselves. I wonder what the medium has to tell them that is so important.

Maggie closes her eyes and takes a deep breath before she resolutely steps onto the opera house's stage. Immediately, the audience erupts partly in cheers, partly in boos. Maggie ignores them all; she is fully focused. Then the woman sends a shockwave of words through the hall: "My sister Kate and I were very young children when this terrible deception began. We were very mischievous children and were just trying to play a trick on our dear, good mother, who was a very skittish woman." She looks out into the audience and the questioning faces of the visitors.

Maggie gives those in attendance a minute to process what they've heard. After all, the star of the world's most famous media family has just opened up to them that her career is based on lies and deception; the religion of spiritualism, of which the Fox Sisters are the founders, and which now has some 8 million followers - all of this is supposed to be based on an out-of-control prank played by two children?

An incredulous silence has settled over the audience like a leaden heaviness. Maggie takes a deep breath and tells the whole story. How she and Kate made up the ghost of the deceased Charles B. Rosna; how the sisters took devilish delight in discovering that their mother was frightened by the evening banging noises; how their mother's fear goaded the girls into banging louder and louder on their bedsteads; how the sisters began tying rope around objects and furniture to move them or make them fall; how they stole apples from the basement of their parents' house and tied string around the fruit. When they were in their beds, they would throw the apples on the floor and quickly pull them under their covers by the string, making rumbling noises that nearly drove their mother mad.

Over time, the sisters found that they could make loud cracking noises with their toe bones. When they did this to their bed frame, it even produced a vibration of the wood. The tapping, he said, was the result of perfect control of the leg muscles below the knee, which send impulses to the tendons of the foot. She says it takes a lot of practice, but then the whole foot can actually be made to tap without the viewer being able to perceive any movement.

Without further ado, Maggie takes off her tights on stage and demonstrates her actual ability to the audience. Another glance at the audience tells her that her critics can't help smirking while the spiritualists are fuming. But she doesn't care. All she cares about is that Kate applauds her courage and that Elisha, wherever he was now, would be proud of his wife. The thought that Leah will also be seething with rage when she gets wind of her performance today gives Maggie a thieving joy. For weeks now, Maggie and Kate have been at bitter odds with her sister.

Although it's a brave and honorable move to clear up the shenanigans, Maggie and Kate haven't made any long-term plans about how they're going to make a living. The only thing they have ever done in their lives was hold seances. Although Maggie receives an honorarium for her confessional appearance and both sisters get some money for newspaper interviews and the publication of a pamphlet entitled: "Death-Blow to Spiritualism," their alcoholism quickly depletes the income.

Some suspect that the money worries are also the reason why Maggie turns to the public again only one year after her confession. She is trying to undo her confession. Critics of the "Fox sisters" found her retraction ridiculous; fans of the media were reassured that they had not been mistaken about Maggie and Kate after all. But it was too late. No one wanted the sisters around anymore; even spiritualists turned their backs on their former leading figures. Maggie makes at least one failed suicide attempt in the years that follow.

Maggie spends the last years of her life in abject poverty. Whether the "Fox Sisters" ever reconciled with Leah is not known.

All three sisters die within short intervals of each other just a few years after the fateful confession. Maggie and Kate are buried in the Brooklyn borough of New York. The two sisters lie side by side in a common grave - just as they once did on those eerie nights in what was probably America's first "haunted house."

THE LESS WE ADMIRE MIRAGES, THE MORE WE ARE ABLE TO ABSORB THE TRUTH.

- Erasmus von Rotterdam (1466-1536),
Renaissance humanist, theologian, and philosopher -

CHAPTER 10

THE PRINCE OF POYAIS

Finley leans on the railing with his arms folded. Cold wind blows in his face, ruffling his brown, shoulder-length curly hair. The man takes a deep breath and sucks the cool, fresh breeze into his lungs. Finley sighs. If only his family could share this exciting adventure with him. But he has had to leave them behind in Scotland's capital, Edinburgh - for now. The shoemaker watches, lost in thought, the white, salty spray dancing across the angry Atlantic. Finley looks forward to his future in the unknown land. The soil there is said to be so fertile that farmers can harvest corn three times a year and grow profitable crops for sugar and tobacco. Revenues in the millions are predicted for industrious farmers. Game and fish are said to be so plentiful that a single day's hunting is enough to feed a family for an entire week. The thriving coastal capital, with its wide, cobbled boulevard lined with magnificent mansions, serves as the center of life for 20,000 people. There is a theater, an opera house, a magnificent cathedral, a bank, parliament buildings, and, of course, the royal palace. His new place of work. For Finley has accepted the post of civil servant and will soon be shoemaker to the princess herself. In a country where people tell each other that "beads of pure gold" float in the rivers there. A smile flits across the Scot's thin-lipped mouth.

"Actually," he thinks to himself, "it sounds too good to be true...".

With a glance into the distance and a quiet sigh, the young shoemaker thinks of the man he has to thank for this and whom heaven must have sent: Gregor MacGregor.

It is Christmas Eve in 1786 when a baby boy sees the light of day on the MacGregor family estate on the north shore of Loch Katrine in Stirlingshire, Scotland. The parents of the newborn Gregor are the captain of the East India Company, Daniel and his wife, Ann. The Roman Catholic family belongs to the Clan Gregor, a Scottish tribe from the Highlands, which has its origins as early as the 9th century. The Gregor clan produces, among others, the Scottish folk hero Rob Roy, Gregor's great-great uncle, and they are known to be among the first Scottish families to begin playing the bagpipes in the early 17th century.

In 1794, Daniel MacGregor dies, leaving his wife Ann with 8-year-old Gregor and his two sisters. The widow gets help from relatives in caring for and raising the three half-orphans. Between 1802 and 1803, the then 15-year-old Gregor is said to have studied at the University of Edinburgh - there is no evidence for this, as the Scotsman does not graduate.

Not much is known about Gregor's childhood. What is certain, however, is that MacGregor's youth ended when he joined the British army in 1803 at the age of sixteen. His family buys him, probably for 450 British pounds (about 50,000 USD), into the position of ensign in the 57th Regiment of Foot. Later, the young man has an engaging personality; his nature is characterized by imagination, daring, and, in addition, he has a good portion of unscrupulousness. But he is also said to be a bon vivant and a man of pleasure.

A turbulent period coincides with the young man's entry into the British army. The self-crowned French emperor, Napoleon, plunges Europe into numerous colonial wars. In the blink of an eye, France rises to become a world power on par with Great Britain from 1802 to 1815. In the turmoil of the war, Gregor is granted a special honor: after less than a year of training, the young soldier is already up for promotion to lieutenant. Other military servants have to do at least three years of work for this. The newly appointed lieutenant spends a few months with the regiment's 1st Battalion on the Norman Island of Guernsey before his transfer to Gibraltar.

The year is 1804, when Lieutenant MacGregor, at the age of 17, meets the attractive daughter of an already deceased admiral of the Royal Navy. But with her delicate features, Maria Bowater is not only extraordinarily pretty to look at - but the young woman also has a considerable dowry. In June 1805, the wedding bells ring in the famous St. Margaret's Church in Westminster, England. After the marriage, the newlyweds reside in London at the estate of Mary's aunt.

Having gained considerable wealth through the marriage, MacGregor decides to buy the rank of captain for 900 British pounds (about 80,000 USD). Normally, a soldier waits seven years for such a promotion unless he has the financial means to buy the rank of captain.

MacGregor's 57th Regiment is stationed on the island of Gibraltar between 1805 and 1809. Gregor, at 5'7", is a handsome figure at the time. He wears his brown, wavy hair in a short hairstyle. Bushy sideburns frame the eighteen-year-olds face on either side, reaching almost to his chin.

MacGregor develops a fascination with high-end uniforms, preferably adorned with rank insignia and lapel medals, while stationed at Gibraltar. This passion, however, is not well received by his subordinate soldiers - Captain MacGregor does not tolerate non-commissioned officers and other crew members leaving their quarters without full-dress uniforms. His troops can't understand why they, too, have to be perfectly dressed all the time just because their leader has a penchant for exquisite military clothing. But they have no choice but to grumble and follow Captain MacGregor's orders.

In 1809, the Duke of Wellington orders the 57th Regiment to Portugal to reinforce the Anglo-Portuguese army. Urgently needed reinforcements to drive the French soldiers out of Spain. MacGregor and his men arrive in Lisbon on July 15, 1809. However, just a few weeks later, Gregor is detached from the 8th Line Battalion of the Portuguese Army. Here the 22-year-old serves as major from October 1809 to April 1810. It is said that MacGregor's withdrawal from Lisbon was ordered only because the lad had fallen out with one of his superiors. The originally trivial conflict is said to have escalated to the point where the higher-ranking captain fought for MacGregor's transfer and quickly got it.

Gregor must have seen this as a severe defeat - he officially withdrew from service in the British Army on May 24, 1810. His superiors even return the 1350 British pounds (about 100,000 USD) that the young man once paid to serve as an ensign and later as a captain. With resignation over the end of his career in the British Army, Gregor returns to his wife, Maria, in Britain. His men of the 57th Regiment, however, fight on relentlessly. MacGregor's former army gains considerable prestige after the battle at the Spanish town of La Albuera on May 16, 1811. The troop of soldiers gets the nickname "Die-Hards." Canister shots seriously wound Lieutenant Colonel William Inglis during the battle. But the brave soldier stubbornly refuses to retreat from the battle. He wants to stand by his soldiers. As the men come under enormous pressure and stress from French attacks, Inglis encourages his men with the words, "Die hard, 57th, die hard!". (In German: "Die hard 57th, die hard!"). MacGregor, who left the 57th Regiment a year before the infamous "Battle of Albuera," will use his former troop's reputation to his advantage every now and then.

Back with his wife Maria, the young couple moves into a house in Edinburgh, Scotland, which MacGregor's mother rents. The 23-year-old gives himself the title of "Colonel" and undeservedly adorns himself with the insignia of a Portuguese knightly order. The former soldier is driven through the streets of Edinburgh in an extravagant carriage. Despite all the effort, he fails to achieve the high social status in the Scottish capital that he so desires.

It is 1811 when Gregor decides to return to England with his wife, Maria. Here he wants to finally make it to the high society of London. The 24-year-old also has what he thinks is a brilliant idea to make his way into the upper class. From now on, the young man puts the noble predicate "Sir" in front of his name. He thinks up fantastic family connections to various dukes, counts, and barons. And Gregor actually succeeds in making a credible and respectable impression on London's high society. The young man thinks he has reached his goal - until Maria suddenly dies in December 1811.

His wife's death changes everything abruptly. With Maria, not only the main source of income of the self-proclaimed nobleman dies, but he also loses the support of the influential family of his dead wife. Does MacGregor mourn Maria's death? Perhaps. But what is certain is that his main concern now is how to make money. The widower's options are limited. An engagement to a well-to-do match shortly after Maria's death could get him into trouble with his dead wife's family - he fears public exposure. Another option would be to return to Scotland. There he could farm his family's lands- but the very thought of this sweaty work makes him shudder. The only professional experience MacGregor has is his military service. But returning to the British Army is not an acceptable option either, given the less-than-praiseworthy circumstances of how he left the force.

But then, as the story goes, a solution to his plight comes to mind - in the form of the Venezuelan revolutionary Francisco de Miranda. The general had distinguished himself in the Venezuelan War of Independence in 1811. When the revolutionary pays a visit to London, the country's upper class celebrates him. MacGregor is not unaware of high society's admiration for the revolutionary. So, Gregor also wants to be courted by the elite. From now on, he, too, will experience exciting adventures in the New World. On his return, he could tell fantastic stories that would bring him the long-awaited fame and admiration of the upper class.

Without further ado, MacGregor sells the small estate in Scotland that he once inherited from his father. With the proceeds from the sale, he finances his passage to South America in 1812. The globetrotter makes a stopover in Jamaica's capital Kingston and finally reaches his destination in April 1812: Venezuela.

Just two weeks before his arrival in the Venezuelan capital, Caracas was struck by destructive earth tremors. 15,000-20,000 people lost their lives on that afternoon of March 26, 1812, when the ground began to shake. The material damage is unquantifiable. In addition to the natural disaster and all the losses it caused, the Venezuelan War of Independence was still raging there at the time. Parts of the South American country are already under the control of the ever-advancing Spanish armies.

MacGregor grasps the seemingly hopeless situation of General Miranda, who is relentlessly fighting for Venezuela's secession from colonial motherland Spain. Gregor offers him his military services. After all, he is a former officer of the British 57th Regiment, better known as the "Die-Hards." The revolutionary is grateful and accepts the young man's offer without hesitation. He puts MacGregor in command of a cavalry battalion and directly gives him the rank of colonel.

Indeed, the 25-year-old colonel and his cavalry manage to rout the enemy force west of the city of Maracay. Although this operation will remain MacGregor's most successful, his superiors are nevertheless pleased with his military achievements.

It is June 10, 1812, when Gregor marries for the second time in Maracay at the age of 25. His bride is Doña Josefa Andrea Aristeguieta y Lovera-known to everyone as just "Josefa." The gorgeous woman comes from a prominent and influential family in Caracas. Her cousin is the famous revolutionary Simón Bolívar, who led numerous occupied South American countries to independence from the Spanish Empire. Perhaps this prestige makes her even more attractive to MacGregor.

June of 1812 is drawing to a close when Miranda, a revolutionary, promotes the 26-year-old MacGregor to brigadier general. But less than four weeks later, Símon Bolívar's enemy troops seize the key port of Puerto Cabello on Venezuela's northern coast. The battle is thus lost, and the Venezuelan Republic has no choice but to surrender.

The Spanish take General Miranda prisoner. MacGregor, his wife, and the pitiful remnants of the leadership escape aboard the two-masted sailing ship "Sapphire" and evacuate to the Dutch Caribbean Island of Curaçao. Símon Bolívar follows them later.

While General Miranda is imprisoned in Spain, Bolívar now leads the Venezuelan independence movement. But the new commander decides to take some time to calmly plan all further steps with a cool head. MacGregor, on the other hand, soon gets bored in Curaçao. He decides to leave the Caribbean Island with his wife. He takes Josefa to Jamaica; Gregor himself travels to General Antonio Nariño's base in Tunja, located in the eastern Colombian Andes. Nariño is one of the first military leaders of the South American Wars of Independence. MacGregor wants to join Nariño's Republican army in New Grenada. With General Miranda as a reference, MacGregor grabs command of a 1,200-man force.

In the years to come, numerous military operations take place under the command of Gregor, who stands out for his courage and leadership. However, he reaps more defeats than successes. Nevertheless, in his stories, he always manages to twist the events in such a way that the listener must believe that the supposed defeat is rather a success.

It is a wild and adventurous time in America for MacGregor and his soldiers. During one of the numerous campaigns, it slowly becomes apparent that Gregor also has a deceitful streak in him. In 1817, MacGregor has a campaign financed by American investors. The shrewd soldier sells the investors an island off the coast of Florida, which at the time is still occupied by Spain and not yet conquered by MacGregor. But with his 50-man squad, he manages to wrest the 47-square-kilometer island from the Spanish soldiers. Gregor proudly proclaims the "Republic of Florida." But MacGregor has no desire to deal with a possible counterattack by the Spanish. In a fly-by-night action, he simply makes off without paying his soldiers.

It is also 1817 when MacGregor becomes a father for the first time at the age of 30. Josefa gives birth to a baby boy in the

Bahamas, in the capital Nassau. The happy parents give their offspring the name Gregorio.

A significant turning point in MacGregor's life is marked by his stay on the Nicaraguan mainland in Central America. The Atlantic Ocean stretches from north to south in an almost unbroken coastline. The region, called the Miskito Coast, is a swampy area that only insects call home after the end of British colonial rule.

But when MacGregor sets eyes on the inhospitable land in April 1820, an idea strikes him. After a night of drinking together, he persuades King George Frederic Augustus to sign over 32,375 square kilometers of the Miskito Coast to him. Gregory pays the old ruler with rum and jewelry. Then the newly crowned landowner returns to Great Britain.

Arriving in London, Sir Gregor MacGregor has become the Prince of Poyais. The Miskito king has appointed him as such. He exaggerates the truth.

The elite like to surround themselves with the apparent nobleman. Dozens of invitations to social events or official receptions reach the family. The MacGregors have arrived in high society. Always at Gregor's side is the new princess of Poyais: his wife with their 3-year-old son Georgio. In the course of 1820, MacGregor's wife Josefa Andrea Aristeguieta gives birth to another little girl at her sister-in-law's house in Ireland. The proud parents named the newborn child after his mother's Christian name: Josefa Anna Gregoria.

London society listens with interest to the exciting stories that the newly appointed prince has to tell about his kingdom of Poyais and its flourishing capital St. Josephs, the pompous mountains stretching into the bluest sky imaginable, and the clearest, purest air you've ever breathed. And MacGregor also tells his listeners about the inland locals, who are very welcoming of British settlement in Poyai. That's also the reason, Gregor explains, why he came to London. He wants to encourage the British to invest in his great empire.

MacGregor begins to stir the advertising wheels for Poyais. The prince gives newspaper interviews, has advertisements and pamphlets produced by publicists hired for the purpose, and ensures that ballads, especially for Poyais, echo through the streets. "We'll go to Poyais together. We'll flood the seas together, to fairer lands and brighter skies..." is heard from the pubs and taverns of London, Edinburgh, and Glasgow. MacGregor also publishes a detailed 355-page guidebook under the pseudonym Captain Thomas Strangeways. A specially created coat of arms and a "traditional" Poya fantasy uniform are also not to be missed, of course.

It doesn't take long for the aggressive advertising campaign for Poyais to have the effect MacGregor wants. The "Prince of Poyais" sells his prospective buyers government bonds worth 200,000 pounds (today around 25 million USD) and offers the unsuspecting the prospect of a return of six percent - twice what British bonds bring in. Those who want to become part of Poyai's flourishing economic miracle can buy land parcels from Prince MacGregor. The price of a piece of land in Poyais is rising rapidly because of the high demand. In addition, MacGregor willingly exchanges all the assets of the soon-to-be emigrants, all genuine English banknotes, into worthless "Poyais dollars" - which he designed and printed himself.

To eager merchants and skilled craftsmen, MacGregor offers free passage. And so it happens that Finley, a Scotsman, also sells his prosperous business, leaves his family behind, and sets off on the long voyage to what is probably the most beautiful and economically prosperous country in the world.

Two large sailing ships with a total of 240 excited settlers set sail at the beginning of 1823. The crossing to Poyais takes two long, monotonous months before the settlers arrive at their destination.

But they seem to have lost their way and dropped anchor in the wrong place. The once hopeful emigrants find themselves standing on a desolate coastline bordered by a dense forest; amidst muddy ground, surrounded by penetrating buzzing mosquitoes that litter their bodies with itchy bites. There is nothing to be seen of St. Joseph's capital far and wide. The locals do not help them; they fight for their daily survival.

A few courageous stranded people, 150 in number, are said to be fighting their way through the impassable forest to reach the interior of the country. They are in search of the Miskito king. When they locate the man and desperately describe their predicament to him, the settlers realize that they have succumbed to a terrible deception. They have lost everything. The only thing they possess now are the worthless Poyais dollars. The Miskito king did not even know that the 240 people were making their way to his land. He had indeed signed the coast over to MacGregor for his use, but he never gave him the title of prince, nor did he allow him to do what he was now doing to the swampy coast. Enraged by the events, the king declares the agreement with the impostor MacGregor invalid with immediate effect and gruffly demands that the settlers subdue. Otherwise, he will be forced to kill each and every one of them.

Resigned, the settlers try to make the best of their bitter situation. They build huts out of rotten wood and leaves. It is not long before the emigrants find themselves in hell on earth. Dirty drinking water makes them sick, severe malnutrition weakens them, and yellow fever sweeps them away. Quite a few of them opt for suicide.

One day, deep despair overcomes Shoemaker Finley. The man has lost everything and plunged his family into misfortune with the dream of a paradisiacal life in Poyais. Soiled clothes cover the numerous mosquito bites on his emaciated body. In his hand, a pistol. He sees no way out, no rescue. The shoemaker sits down on the marshy shore and stares at the Atlantic. Silent tears roll down his cheeks. As if in slow motion, he brings the gun to his right temple with his right hand. Then, with his eyelids pressed together, he takes one last desperate deep breath and pulls the trigger.

What Finley could not have foreseen: only a short time later, rescue approaches. A ship picks up the desperate stranded and takes them to Belize in Central America. From here, the last survivors, braving disease, and starvation, begin their journey back to Britain. The sad result of the trickster MacGregor: of the 240 settlers, only 60 escape with their lives. A few of them still do not believe that MacGregor could have tricked them - they tell themselves it must be a misunderstanding. Perhaps their belief in a mistake will help them not to dwell on their fate. In the coming weeks and months, the press in Great Britain will report extensively on the outrages of Gregor MacGregor.

Even before the few survivors of MacGregor's fantasy land return in October 1823, he takes off. The crook flees with his family to Paris, France. It must be 1824 when mother Josefa gives birth to their third child in the family's lavish home on the Champs-Élysées. They give the little boy the name Constantino. Here in France, MacGregor, a man of pleasure, lives a genteel life.

An old saying goes, "If you're greedy for money, you'll never be full." And MacGregor simply can't get enough, either. In France, he also spreads the legend of Poyais Paradise and tries to sell government bonds and land - this time worth 300,000 pounds (about 40 million USD). But unlike in Great Britain, the French authorities notice that their citizens are submitting applications to leave the country in rows for a country that does not exist. So, they track down the swindler MacGregor and prevent worse by arresting him.

The swindler soon finds himself before a French court for fraud. Here his manipulative skills and his talent for inventing tall tales seem to be impressively demonstrated - because MacGregor convinces the court of his innocence in the whole misery. In the summer of 1826, the verdict is handed down against the self-proclaimed prince: Acquittal!

MacGregor returns to London with his wife and children, where the excitement about his brazen deception slowly begins to subside. Rumor has it that he was also arrested in London but released after a week without being charged. The former bon vivant and his family keep their heads above water with all sorts of scams, albeit on a smaller scale. All the money MacGregor took from the people for the government bonds of his fantasy country, he had spent with full hands. Not only did he have to finance the large-scale advertising campaign for "Poyais," but his lifestyle of good food, expensive cigars, lavish receptions, and high-quality clothing was not cheap either. So even the smaller scams, such as the pitiful attempt to sell certificates again, which entitled the purchaser to use a piece of land in "Poyais" for five shillings (about 3000 USD) per acre (about 4050 square meters), could no longer fill MacGregor's wallet.

In May 1838, Gregor's wife, Josefa MacGregor, dies near Edinburgh. The widower, now 51 years old, is drawn to Venezuela after the death of his wife. It was already in 1823 when the last Spanish commanders-in-chief saw themselves forced to capitulate - thus officially ending the Venezuelan War of Independence. MacGregor, now impoverished, cleverly arranged for his former military rank in the Venezuelan army to be restored - he now had outstanding pay for his military service and a decent pension.

On December 4, 1845, just a few days before his 58th birthday, the "King of the Financial Swindlers" dies in Venezuela's capital, Caracas, on the edge of the Caribbean Sea-not far from the muddy coast MacGregor once fantasized about as an economic miracle. If nothing else, his gift for telling fantastic stories and his engaging charm ensured that he garnered recognition and admiration throughout his life. But the impostor was also hated and disliked because of his fraud. However, it is not known whether there were people who wanted to kill MacGregor.

There is also no record of how the lives of MacGregor's sons, Gregorio and Constantinos, progressed. It can be assumed that the children of the impostor lived in Scotland. Only daughter Josefa is known to have died in 1872. She left two sons, but they remained childless throughout her life, so it is not known whether there are any direct descendants of MacGregor.

The journalist David Sinclair is so fascinated by the vision of the impostor, his energy and determination, but also by MacGregor's almost pathological overconfidence that he digs through all the documents that still exist - he can even get hold of the only copy of the "Poyais Travel Guide" from 1822 that is still in circulation via a British bookseller. In 2004, Sinclair publishes a detailed biography of MacGregor entitled: "The Land That Never Was: Sir Gregor MacGregor and History's Boldest Deception," in which he critically examines some of the tales the con man himself has circulated about himself. MacGregor's manipulatively told invented stories about his work, nevertheless, continues to show assertiveness today.

Thus, one can still read in some publications that the impostor allegedly once recorded great military victories.

To this day, the story of the impostor who invented an entire country continues to fascinate. Although, even after MacGregor, other swindlers deprive people of their savings by selling non-existent real estate to trusting victims, Gregor MacGregor remains the only financial swindler in history to have invented an entire country, including the status of nobility.

» *A FLATTERER IS A FRIEND WHO IS INFERIOR TO YOU OR PRETENDS TO BE.* **«**

- *Aristoteles (384 B.C.-322 B.C.),*
Greek philosopher and naturalist -

CHAPTER 11

THE ROMANIAN BOX

The sound of the sea is muffled from far away. This sound has been his daily companion for years, his only comfort in this goddamned hell. At the same time, it reminds him of the dangers that lurk beyond these walls of reinforced concrete. The sea is usually calm, but from one moment to the next, it can turn into a raging monster. The waves then crash high against the rocks as if trying to bury the island beneath them.

At night, the sea is even more sinister. The black waves seem endless, and the surf is deafeningly loud. Some say that the sea off Alcatraz is cursed and that the soul of every prisoner who dared to escape was lost in it.

The man drops the newspaper in his lap and stares dreamily out the window of the Hôtel de Crillon, draped with heavy velvet curtains. It is a glorious morning in the spring of 1925; the people of Paris are enjoying the first rays of the day's sun. Passersby sit hunched over their morning newspaper in the numerous cafés along the boulevards. Some are smoking a cigarette, casually exchanging a few words with the person sitting next to them or observing the hustle and bustle of the street. The warm air is filled with the scent of the trees, and many a person wears his jacket over his arm on his way to work.

In the 16th district of the capital of France stretches the Place du Trocadéro with its palace of the same name. The building, reminiscent of a church due to its twin towers, stands on the other bank of the Seine opposite a red-colored steel structure - the Eiffel Tower. Both buildings were erected in the last century in the course of the World's Fair and are considered landmarks of Paris. Now, some 50 years later, one of them is to be razed to the ground.

Through the bluish haze of his cigarette smoke, the black-and-white photograph of the Eiffel Tower can be seen on the newsprint. Primroses and tulips bloom on the field of Mars at the foot of the impressive steel scaffolding with its "Citroen" neon sign. Despite the idyll, the article below speaks of the slow decay of the tower.

Completed by Gustave Eiffel in 1889, the structure must be repainted every seven years due to the constant threat of rust - all by hand. The renovation work, which takes up to 18 months, consumes around 60 tons of paint. This results in enormous costs, which raises the question of whether one should continue to put this high effort into preserving the Eiffel Tower or whether demolishing the structure would not be better.

As he skims the article several times, the man's hand slides to the secret pockets of his jacket. He originally had these pockets sewn into his jacket so that he could deposit his winnings from card games on ocean liners. Now, however, the profits are dwindling ever faster, forcing the man to think of new methods. And so, he recalls a conversation he had years ago with a contractor in Kansas City, USA. He mentioned that there was a lot of money to be made from demolition work and the resulting scrap iron.

His gaze glides from the newspaper to the window again. Inside him, an idea is slowly growing about how to turn the massive steel structure into a source of money for him.

In the days that follow, he finds out about possible ironmongers in the area and scams stationery from the Paris Post Office to make business cards. He wants to pose as the deputy director of the Post and Telegraph Ministry and offer the Eiffel Tower for sale and demolition. A delicate matter, after all, his venture could attract a lot of attention and thus be doomed to failure.

When he has found six suitable scrap dealers, he asks them to maintain the utmost secrecy. The city, he says, does not want to cause a stir since it does not want the public to know what the French government intends to do with the famous landmark.

When the men arrive in Paris a week later, a limousine is waiting for them in front of the Hôtel de Crillon, in which the troupe is taken to the Eiffel Tower. The alleged director of the Ministry of Posts leads them to the ticket booth, pulls out a business card, and is allowed to pass with the six civil engineers thanks to his high position. The ticket seller cannot suspect that behind the facade of the sovereign appearing man is, in truth, a fraud.

Victor Lustig was born on January 4, 1890, in Arnau, a town in the Kingdom of Bohemia. At that time, his family belonged to the upper social class. His father, Ludwig, is a pipe and tobacco merchant and, on top of that, the mayor of Arnau, which is why his parents are confident about the boy's future. A solid lawyer is to be made of the young Victor, which is why they send him to the best schools along the Elbe and then to the Sorbonne in Paris. Even then, the first thoughts of demolishing the Eiffel Tower were already buzzing through the heads of the

Parisian government. Despite his good education, Lustig had to serve a two-month sentence in prison at the age of 18. It is not known why he went off the rails, but from then on, the boy's criminal career slowly took off.

Between 1909 and 1912, he served several prison sentences for fraud in Vienna, Klagenfurt, and Zurich, and even the city of love could not dissuade him from his criminal activities. At night, the 19-year-old hangs out in poker and billiard halls, learning the tricks of the gambling trade. In the course of this, Lustig soon discovers a new, lucrative source of income: Overseas trips between Europe and the USA. Here, rich businessmen pass the time with games of chance and cards. Together with his new acquaintance, the con artist Nicky Arnstein, Lustig wants to exploit this circumstance to scam his way into big money. One of their tricks, for example, is to let their fellow gamblers talk them into gambling. Lustig and Arnstein are reserved and pretend that they "don't really feel like it.

For years, the two are successful with this business model, but with the start of the First World War in 1914, the transatlantic voyages disappear, and with them, the secure source of money. Lustig now has to come up with something new and, two years after the end of the war, dares to take a desperate step: to escape the threat of bankruptcy, he travels to the land of unlimited opportunity - the United States. Thanks to his outstanding knowledge of human nature and his elegance, the now 30-year-old soon moves into wealthy circles there and gives himself the title of nobility. As "Count Victor Lustig," he continues his frauds in the future and seeks out people who have just come into a lot of money through their business. These are not yet so experienced in dealing with their wealth and can easily fall into his traps.

But as easy as the life of an impostor may seem to the outside world, the danger of being exposed is omnipresent. Time and again, Lustig's new acquaintances ask him what he actually does for a living. The alleged count then shows them a box, which he calls a "Romanian box."To demonstrate his source of income, he removes the lid, puts a 100-dollar bill inside, closes the box, and claims that complicated chemical processes are now copying the bill inside. The waiting time for this is supposed to be several hours - enough time for Lustig to do something with the curious businessmen and to talk to them. In doing so, he follows ten rules that he has determined:

1. Be a patient listener.
2. Never look bored.
3. Wait until your counterpart reveals his political opinion, and then agree with him.
4. Let your counterpart reveal his religious views and then have the same.
5. Suggest a conversation about sex. However, do not pursue it until your counterpart has expressed interest in it.
6. Never talk about illness unless special concern is shown.
7. Never interfere in your counterpart's personal circumstances.
8. Boasting is taboo. Let your importance be felt in silence.
9. Always be neat and tidy.
10. Do not get drunk.

When the troupe returns to the "Romanian box" a short time later, the $100 bill has miraculously doubled in value. Lustig hands the bill to his acquaintances and instructs them to have its authenticity confirmed at a bank. After the businessmen comply with the request and the money actually turns out to be genuine, they are delighted. The alleged count now receives countless offers to purchase the "Romanian box," but the count explains that his copy is a unique item that is not for sale. By using this tactic, he is able to drive up the price until he finally gives in at around 40,000 dollars and sells the thing.

In truth, the "Romanian box" is nothing more than an ordinary wooden box. But then, where did the copied dollar bill appear from? For the demonstration, Lustig obtained a second banknote with a similar serial number, on which he matched the digits in detail by hand. However, since a bank would have noticed the counterfeit, Lustig secretly slipped the real bill to the businessmen for verification.

When the "Romanian box" buyers notice the fraud, they want to confront the impostor. But before they can do so, the impostor has long since made off with the excuse that it supposedly takes around twelve to eighteen hours for the revolutionary money-printing machine to be ready for use again. The trick is ingenious in that no one who has just acquired an apparatus for counterfeiting money would go to the police.

Victor Lustig tours the United States for five years using this method and scams himself out of large sums of money. In 1925, however, he yearns for Europe and returns to Paris. During his abstinence, the city of love has changed a lot. Due to the effect of the second industrial revolution, France is experiencing an economic boom. Among other things, the last hackney carriages gave way to the automobile, and instead of flickering gas lamps, electric lanterns now illuminate the streets.

At this time, the demand for steel and iron also increases. Production is important for national self-esteem, and thanks to the Treaty of Versailles, France quickly becomes the king of exports. Several million tons of steel, cast iron, and pig iron find their way to other countries in the early 1920s, and the automotive industry at home also demands raw materials. So, who wouldn't want to export around 7,000 tons of steel? The only drawback is that a Parisian landmark would have to suffer.

The Eiffel Tower sways slightly in the wind as the six men climb the narrow steps. They have a breathtaking view of the Seine, the Place du Trocadéro, and the colorful hustle and bustle of the people in the Parisian streets, who seem like ants. You can also feel the enormous mass of the steel structure, whose individual girders weigh up to three tons and are held together by a total of 2.5 million rivets.

All five scrap dealers are inwardly calculating the dismantling of the 300-meter-high structure and are gradually beginning to get greedy for money. This is exactly what Victor Lustig has been waiting for - a fierce battle among his potential buyers for the highest sum. But the con man has known for a long time who he ultimately wants to award the contract to.

The man's name is André Poisson. He is the owner of a small, little-known business and fulfills a decisive condition: just like Lustig's American friends, he has only just come into money and is, therefore, very insecure in the world of the rich. Lustig has already registered this in his shaky handshake upon greeting him. In addition, the scrap dealer is held back by his wife when doing business. She advises him to think carefully about deals and weigh all options. Not an easy decision for Poisson, for whom dismantling the Eiffel Tower could give his business a boost. Lustig makes this circumstance his own and tricks the scrap dealer at another meeting in private.

The impostor makes him believe that his financial situation as a civil servant is "really bad" at the moment. He would indeed sell Poisson the building, but only on the condition that the latter would have to give him a little money on the quiet. The scrap dealer takes the bait and now has no doubts whatsoever about the deal - after all, a swindler wouldn't ask him for even more money for bribery purposes.

And so, Poisson hands Lustig not only the amount for the purchase of the Eiffel Tower but also an envelope with extra money. The impostor makes off with the proud total sum of one million francs (about 200,000 USD today). He travels by train to Vienna, goes into hiding there, and checks the front pages of the French newspapers every day, expecting to read a headline about his latest deception - in vain. The days pass, and there is not even a hint of a report anywhere that the Eiffel Tower has been sold to a previously unknown scrap dealer. Had the reporters possibly been instructed to keep quiet so as not to jeopardize the search for the fugitive? Are they already on his trail?

Meanwhile, in Paris, a curious scene presents itself to the real officials of the Post Ministry: a man named André Poisson enters the building and holds the signed purchase papers for the Eiffel Tower under the noses of the befuddled employees. When he is emphatically assured that the world-famous landmark is neither for sale nor a certain "Count Lustig" employed at the Post Office, it dawns on the poor scrap dealer he has probably been had. He does not call the police, however, because he is too ashamed of the impostor's perfidy. Who would still take him for a full person if he went public with the story?

Victor Lustig is unaware of all this. Since he no longer feels safe in Vienna, his escape route once again takes him across the pond to the United States, where he joins forces with an old acquaintance named William Watts - at the time, one of the most renowned money counterfeiters in the USA. During Lustig's first stay, the duo already went after joint scams involving counterfeit whiskey labels. Now they make use of Watts' knowledge again and rent a workshop to produce counterfeit money. They succeed in doing this in such a deceptively genuine way that the counterfeits cannot easily be distinguished from real money. In this way, the pair put millions of fake dollars into circulation in no time at all. It is even said that fifty percent of the counterfeit money circulating in the US at the time comes from Lustig and his accomplice.

As successful as this scheme is, it soon attracts the attention of the Secret Service. How the authorities ultimately succeed in exposing Lustig and Watts is not known. Still, the duo is arrested in 1931 after a trip to Mexico, Texas, and interrogated in Remsen County, Oklahoma, by Sheriff Miller. Lustig, however, does not want to spend his twilight years in jail under any circumstances and does what he has done all his life. During the interrogation, he uses his tried and tested rules and is able to elicit from the policeman that he is suffering from money problems.

Immediately, a feeling of satisfaction spreads inside Lustig. Jackpot! Not only has he gained Miller's trust, but he already has an idea of how to persuade the poor sheriff to make a deal. And so, the con man tells him about a special wooden box with which money can be produced within a few hours. Lustig explains that he has locked the "Romanian box," as he calls it, somewhere at the train station and instructs Miller to pick it up. Instead of questioning the story and viewing it as a possible bribery attempt, the sheriff goes and retrieves the box in question. After a fake demonstration by Lustig, he is so thrilled that he promptly pays him $25,000 for it. Despite his financial problems, the handsome sum poses no problem for him - after all, he can now copy vast amounts of money.

The con man's plan succeeds. Miller releases Lustig, who, on the other hand, leaves the sheriff in the belief that he has got rid of his worries in one fell swoop. A classic win-win situation. Soon, however, the policeman realizes that he has been hoodwinked. Unlike the businessmen, who are ashamed of their reputation, he goes in search of the impostor, tracks him down in Chicago, and demands his money back at gunpoint. On the other hand, Lustig remains calm and claims that the "Romanian box" is surely just broken. He assures the sheriff that he will fix it and, on top of that, hands him $50,000 as a sign that he is "really serious." Miller agrees and takes the money - not suspecting that it is also counterfeit.

Victor Lustig has escaped justice once again and seems to have reached the zenith of his untouchability. He is an excellent actor, knows how to get to the right people through his knowledge of human nature, and people trust him blindly. While the Nozière case dominates the headlines of the newspapers, Lustig, after escaping from Miller, is able to continue his scams in the USA unhindered for four years. Then, the Secret Service is on his heels again. With a special unit, the impostor is finally to be put out of circulation - with success. In 1935, Lustig is arrested and unhesitatingly confesses to some of his deeds but does not reveal where exactly his accomplice is producing the printing plates for the fake dollar bills.

He is housed in the 108-meter-high "US federal house of Detention" in Manhattan, which is considered escape-proof to date. Only four months after his arrest, Lustig proves the opposite: with bed sheets knotted together, he climbs out of his cell and pretends to clean the windows of the bronze-colored building. As soon as his feet hit the ground, he runs away. This time, however, he can't enjoy his freedom for long because just

29 days later, he is arrested again in Pittsburgh, Pennsylvania. At that moment, the con man realizes that things can't go smoothly for him forever. Sooner or later, the gripping teeth of the handcuffs snap shut - no matter how many steps you think you are ahead of the cops.

No sooner is he back in custody than Lustig is put on trial on December 5, 1935. The judge sentences him to twenty years in prison for producing over 2 million dollars in counterfeit money. He is to serve his sentence in what is probably the most famous and safest prison in the world: Alcatraz. 8.5 hectares in size, 41-meter-high cliffs, and located in the middle of an ocean bay off San Francisco. Anyone who dares to attempt an escape here must face the dangers of the raging ocean tides. Assuming he even manages to get past the guards and reinforced concrete facades.

The prison houses some of the most dangerous criminals in the US at the time, including Al Capone. Incredible as it may sound, the notorious mobster and Lustig have a common past, in which the conman managed to cheat Capone out of several $10,000.

The incident took place several years before Lustig's arrest. The Eiffel Tower had been sold, the con man had moved to the USA, and his business of doubling money was in full swing. He now tried to bring this to the bigwigs of the criminal world. However, he didn't want to sell them his invention. He intended to cheat them as well. Lustig gained Capone's trust, borrowed 50,000 dollars from him, and promised to double it within a few weeks. Capone gave him the money but still advised him to be careful. After all, Lustig knew who he was dealing with.

In fact, the con man merely deposited the money in a locker, let some time pass, and then returned with the $50,000 in hand. Unfortunately, he had not managed to double the sum, was his explanation. Capone was so taken aback by his honesty that he refrained from punishing him and gave Lustig $5,000 for his courage. After all, it should not be up to him if the failed man had to die impoverished. Whether the swindler speculated on Capone's generosity or whether the matter became too hot for him, and he returned the money to the dreaded man is unknown. But the simultaneous imprisonment of the men has, in any case, resulted in the notorious mobster keeping his protective hand over Lustig.

Capone's guardianship, however, cannot affect Lustig's health, which deteriorates rapidly in the mid-1940s. He falls ill with pneumonia and is transferred to the prison hospital in Springfield, Missouri. There the former fraud genius passes away on March 11, 1947, but the public will not learn of his passing until two years later for reasons unknown.

To this day, Lustig's sale of the Eiffel Tower remains unrivaled. Although imitators tried to sell off Buckingham Palace or the Statue of Liberty, none of them managed to hold a candle to Lustig's brilliance.

The cityscape of Paris undergoes rapid modernization after the Second World War. Some buildings and streets are adapted to the needs of the growing population and the progress of technology. In addition, developments such as the construction of residential buildings in the suburbs and the expansion of the public transport network are implemented to meet the Parisian population's needs and solve the city's traffic problems.

On the other hand, the glittering reflection of the Eiffel Tower can still be admired by people today in the peaceful rippling waters of the Seine.

» **THE SMALL ROGUES ARE LOCKED UP; THE BIG ONES ARE HATED.** «

- Swabian proverb -

CHAPTER 12

FINE FEATHERS MAKE FINE BIRDS

(Reading sample from the book "True Crime Germany 2")

It is 1849, and while Guiseppe Mazzini proclaims the Roman Republic in the Papal States, the revolution that began in March 1848 continues to keep the population of the German Confederation in suspense.

In the midst of all this political unrest, Friedrich-Wilhelm Voigt was born on February 13, 1849, in Tilsit, East Prussia. His father, Johann Carl Christian Voigt, a master shoemaker, was fencing under the rule of Emperor Wilhelm I in Baden at the time.

Participation in military campaigns is something of a tradition in the Voigt family. Frederich-Wilhelm's grandfathers had already been part of the campaigns in the years 1813 to 1815, and the boy also developed a liking for the military at an early age, not least because it was common practice in his hometown of Tilsit for a boy to start playing soldier as soon as he could walk. In addition, the Voigt family's apartment is in a favorable location, directly opposite the barracks of the 1st Lithuanian Dragoon Regiment. Thus, it happens that between Friedrich-Wilhelm and the respective crew of the regiment, a friendly contact is established, which enables him to gain service knowledge when he is still a boy. The family looks to Frederich-Wilhelm's future with confidence, hoping that he can use the army as a springboard to attain a respected civil service position.

Crucial to the boy's development above all is his "Uncle Patzig," the first husband of a sister of Friedrich-Wilhelm's mother. This uncle, a mechanic by trade and a man of much knowledge, teaches his nephew reading, arithmetic, and writing even before he enters school, giving Friedrich-Wilhelm a considerable advantage over his classmates when he enters the local, three-grade town school in 1855. In 1858, he transfers to the secondary school.

Until then, the growing child's life seems to be characterized by prosperity, but this changes abruptly when Friedrich-Wilhelm reaches adolescence. One of the triggers for this is the recurring domestic violence of his father, who, after the early death of Uncle Patzig, develops an affinity for gambling and is regularly ripped off by other gamblers. Although this causes the family's fortune to dwindle from time to time and threatens to ruin their existence, the father cannot be dissuaded from his passion; much more, the family tries to keep their precarious financial situation hidden from the outside world as best they can.

In order to escape the "domestic scenes," as Friedrich-Wilhelm titles the tense family idyll, he often leaves the parental home secretly. He seeks shelter with his relatives in Königsberg, 110 kilometers away. During these excursions, he repeatedly came into conflict with law enforcement officers until he was caught stealing for the first time at the age of 14 and was sentenced to two weeks in prison by the Tilsit District Court in 1863.

Since he now had a criminal record, Friedrich-Wilhelm was not allowed to continue attending school and had to find an alternative - which he found in his father's profession. As a journeyman shoemaker, Friedrich-Wilhelm also undertakes years of travel, which takes him through large parts of Pomerania and Brandenburg. However, even during these adventures, he is unable to tear himself away from his criminal activities. In 1867, at the age of 18, he is sentenced to twelve years in prison for forging documents.

After serving his sentence, Friedrich-Wilhelm Voigt was not even free for a year before he committed document forgery again in 1889 and, shortly afterward, even a robbery: with a crowbar, he plundered the court treasury in the Prussian district of Wongrowitz. This offense landed him in prison "for grand larceny" - this time for fifteen years.

When Voigt served his last prison sentence for the time being in 1906, the native of Tilsit was already 57 years old and had spent more than half of his life behind bars.

However, Friedrich-Wilhelm intends to leave his old life behind and earn his money in an "honest way." To do this, he doesn't even want to try to find a job in the German Reich but instead wants to make a new start in Austria-Hungary or Russia. There is only one problem: Voigt needs a passport for his plan, but he is denied one because of his criminal record.

Therefore, he first moves to Wismar in Mecklenburg, where he tries his luck with the court shoemaker Hillbrecht. Soon, however, he is expelled from the Duchy of Mecklenburg-Schwerin and finally arrives in Berlin-Rixdorf, where his sister Bertha gives him shelter in her apartment. He even found work there in the felt shoe factory Albert Viereck, but the authorities constantly watched him. As a result, in August 1906, the police issued Voigt a ban on staying in the greater Berlin area "as a precaution." This ended the shoemaker's dream of "continuing to work honestly" and perhaps one day setting up a shoe store in Bernau for the Wismar court supplier.

Nevertheless, Voigt defied the residence ban and stayed as a "sleeping boy" in unregistered lodgings in Berlin-Friedrichshain near the Silesian train station. At first, he retained his job in the shoe factory, but due to his illegal status, he had no future prospects there and resigned at the beginning of October 1906.

Since the authorities still refused to give him an identity card, Voigt devised a perfidious plan to gain possession of such a document: He wants to disguise himself as a captain and march into the rooms of authority with some soldiers in tow. There, he wants to gain power over the authorities and use a pretext to scam the necessary form in order to end his illegal residence status. The "Köpenickiade" is born.

In devising his scheme, the shoemaker is inspired above all by writer Heinrich Von Kleist, who impressively describes his campaign against the authorities in his novella "Michael Kohlhaas. Since Voigt also feels betrayed by justice, he wants to create a memorial with his rogue play. So, he buys a somewhat shabby but at the same time well-preserved captain's uniform from the junk dealer Bertold Remlinger in Potsdam.

He chose the town hall in Köpenick as the setting, not because of any special historical background, but because the town seems to him to be easiest to reach from his hideout by train. And there is another reason for the choice of the town hall because Voigt is by no means merely interested in regaining his passport. Since, as a newly unemployed man, he is threatened with running out of money, he wants to raid the safe in the Köpenick town hall. It is said to contain two million marks.

But Voigt's coup, against his knowledge, is doomed to failure before it has even begun - because passports are issued at the district administration office, not at a town hall.

In order not to run the risk of being observed in his disguise by other residents of the house and possibly being exposed, Voigt puts on the ankle-length, gray captain's uniform with the blue collar, the thick buttons, and the white belt with golden buckle in his apartment early in the morning of October 16, 1906, and steps out onto the deserted street at around 3:30 am.

First, Voigt takes the 4:00 am train to Köpenick at the Schlesischer Bahnhof to take stock of the situation there. The magnificent town hall, a brick castle with a Gothic-style clock tower completed in 1905, is located in the center of Köpenick's old town, which was built in the 12th century and sits on an island between the Dahme and Spree rivers.

After gathering all the information, the fake captain returns to Berlin around six o'clock. He stays there for a few hours and then takes a cab to Wedding, a district of Berlin, where he has lunch in a garden restaurant. On the way there, Voigt meets a major of the airship division and has to fear for his cover for a few minutes. However, the major does not seem to notice anything unusual; the disguise works.

After lunch, the fake captain vagabonds around Seestraße for some time until he finally meets a troop of Fusiliers of the Guards Fusilier Regiment, nicknamed "Maybugs," in the connecting street Sylterstraße. Voigt seizes the opportunity and orders the company, in a strong East Prussian accent, to "Halt!". The corporal stands at attention and makes the prescribed report to the false captain about the "where from" and "where to." According to the report, his four-man unit was on its way back to the barracks from guard duty at the military swimming pool at Plötzensee. Voigt informs the assembled squad in a sharp tone that they are not allowed to march to the barracks now, as they would be ordered by him to another service by higher command. He then instructs the corporal to summon a second squad of relieved guardsmen from the 4th Guards Regiment on foot, which the latter does without hesitation.

When the second guard team has also approached and reported to their leader Voigt, the false captain orders the first guard commander to the commander of the whole, lets him rank the team, and orders the second commander to the end of the squad. Then Voigt gives the order to march off.

Since he had allegedly not succeeded in "requisitioning" motor vehicles, the false captain led his troop, now eleven strong, to Putlitzstraße station and bought tickets for the Berlin light rail, which took them in the direction of Köpenick. At a stopover in Rummelsburg, Voigt buys the soldiers a beer since they had not returned to the barracks after their guard duty and thus had no opportunity to refresh themselves; he himself treats himself to a cognac for 25 pfennigs. When the train then arrives in Köpenick in the early afternoon, the false captain presses a mark into the hand of each of his men and lets them have lunch in the station restaurant for fifteen minutes while he strolls up and down the corridor.

At the appointed time, Voigt summons the team back to the front of the station building to complete a duty roster for the upcoming coup at the town hall. The fake captain declares that he will "arrest the mayor and perhaps other gentlemen," then has the soldiers fix bayonets to remind them that they are "not commanded for pleasure, but for duty." He does not consider instructions for the treatment of individuals necessary since experience has taught him that anyone who has served even one year knows how to treat an arrestee.

Arriving at the town hall, Voigt first sets up posts around the building. He decreed that the "cockchafers" should man the three portals of the town hall with one sentry each. Voigt orders an off-duty local gendarme, who is loitering on the front steps, to "return to duty immediately" and to assist the troop leader, to whom he gives command of the town hall.

Voigt chooses all his orders and commands with such calmness and composure that no one even suspects that the entire action could be faked. And the longer his plan seems to work, the more the false captain, who had to give in and hide from the authorities his entire life, grows into his role.

Before he goes inside the town hall, Voigt explicitly tells his protégés that no one is allowed to leave or enter the town hall without his order. At about 3:30 pm, with six grenadiers of the 4th Guards Regiment and a fusilier in tow, he marches to the second floor, directly to the office of the chief town clerk, Rosenkranz.

When the fake captain opens the door, Rosenkranz is sitting behind his desk, calmly processing papers. Voigt tells him to get ready to leave immediately, as Voigt has orders to take him to the Neue Wache in Berlin. Rosenkranz follows the instructions without resistance, whereupon the false captain goes to the adjoining study of the mayor of Köpenick, Dr. Georg Langerhans. The mayor is initially surprised by the entourage's visit but then jumps up in horror when he recognizes the rank of the false captain. The latter informs him that he has to arrest him "by the highest order" and take him to the Neue Wache in Berlin.

The flabbergasted Dr. Langerhans inquires about the reason for his arrest, whereupon Voigt tries to brush him off: he himself does not know the exact reason, and the mayor would find out everything "there." But Dr. Langerhans does not let up and demands that the captain show him some "official document" that legitimizes his arrest. Voigt barks that his legitimation is his soldiers and threatens the rebellious man with imprisonment if he continues to defy his majesty's orders. The mayor surrenders to his fate.

To add further power to his authority, Voigt orders two of his soldiers to stand guard at the mayor's side while he himself goes to the cashier's room on the first floor. On his way there, Voigt makes a detour to the office of police inspector Jäckel, whom he finds asleep in his armchair. After Voigt has woken him up, the false captain inquires whether the city of Köpenick pays Jäckel to sit around and slumber. He should have the goodness to go out to ensure the necessary order on the streets in front of the town hall. The police inspector immediately obeys the order of the "captain" but returns a few minutes later, puzzled and equally distraught. He is refused exit; he stammers and asks the false captain to give him leave of absence. Since Voigt feels this is urgently needed, he grants the man his leave, whereupon he disappears to take a bath.

In the cashier's room, Voigt confronts Rendant von Wiltburg with a fait accompli: the mayor of the city of Köpenick is under arrest, and he, the captain, has the power of command over the city hall. Voigt instructs the treasurer to make the cash balance and explains to him that he has to confiscate the stock of the city treasury due to "irregularities in the sewerage works currently being carried out in Köpenick."

After the treasurer has meticulously counted and recalculated the money, which has to be fetched from the local post office, among other places, there are exactly 4,002 marks and 37 pfennigs that end up in small bags, which the false captain has fetched and sealed. Voigt signs a receipt requested by the governor with the name of his last prison governor, "von

Mahlzahn," and the addition "H.i.1.G.R.". - Captain in the 1st Guards Regiment. Finally, Voigt had his prisoners brought to Berlin in hackney carriages; a soldier of the Guard Fusilier Regiment served as an escort. Voigt himself stayed behind.

When the convoy arrived at the Neue Wache, they looked at confused faces. After all, no one there knows anything about an alleged military occupation of the town hall in Köpenick, including the arrest of the mayor. Gradually, it dawns on those involved that they have fallen victim to fraud. However, all attempts to track down the fake captain fail because Voigt has long since made off with his loot. After completing his action, he had given the guards at the town hall money for beer, sausages, and return tickets and ordered them to hold the fort for another half hour. Then he had gone to Köpenick station to return to Berlin on the next train. Before that, he had a glass of beer served to him in the station restaurant, which he emptied "in one go."

Once in Berlin, Voigt got rid of his uniform, stowed it in a cardboard box, and bought a suit, coat, and hat from the best men's outfitter; he paid for the clothes with a thousand-mark bill. Then he resumes his old rank in civilian life and disappears into the hustle and bustle of the big city.

Meanwhile, news of the siege of the town hall in Köpenick spreads like wildfire, and soon the farce of the false captain is known far beyond the borders of the country. The first picture postcards and caricatures can already be purchased the day after the crime, and flyers with special reports are distributed on the streets.

The East Prussian authoritarian state becomes a worldwide public laughingstock: "The whole of Germany is laughing at this," newspapers headline gloatingly on the front page. Even

Emperor Wilhelm II is said to have called Voigt a "genius." Nevertheless, the emperor was no longer willing to put up with the blasphemies and, without further ado, offered a high reward for the capture of the villain.

After only a few days, the authorities receive a decisive clue. A scoundrel named Kallenberg reports that his former cellmate Friedrich-Wilhelm Voigt once confided in him that he was planning such a coup as soon as he was released.

When the police present a photo of Voigt from his criminal file to the staff of the Köpenick city hall, they immediately recognize him. Thus, the identity of the false captain is finally clarified - and Kallenberg is richer by a whopping 3000 marks. But one question remains unsolved: Where is the guy?

He can't have completely vanished into thin air because passers-by find at least his uniform on the grounds of Berlin Tempelhof Airport. But even if this does not lead the police to the desired success, there is still no trace of the false captain.

When the police finally arrived at Voigt's sister's home in Rixdorf, where Voigt was still registered, the woman proved extremely cooperative. She provided the policemen with the address to Voigt's hideout - a direct hit that the police could hardly believe. On the morning of October 26, 1906, ten days after his racket, Voigt is arrested. Another five weeks later, on December 1, 1906, the false captain had to stand trial before the Third Criminal Chamber of District Court II in Berlin on charges of unauthorized exercise of a public office, unauthorized wearing of a uniform, fraud, forgery of documents and unlawful deprivation of liberty.

During the trial, which journalists from all over the world accompany, it turns out that Voigt was never in the army and acquired his military knowledge in early childhood. So how had he managed to deceive every member of the "Köpenickiade"?

Even Mayor Dr. Georg Langerhans, an inveterate reserve officer, had not noticed that the fake captain was, firstly, too old - the age limit for the rank of "captain" at that time was 56, but Voigt was already 57 -secondly, spoke a strong dialect, and his uniform had several flaws, such as a false cockade on his cap.

The reason for the success of his charade was Voigt's self-confident appearance and the dashing tone with which he barked the commands. In retrospect, all involved can consider themselves lucky that it remained at a simple arrest because the soldiers testify in court that they would have used their bayonets and firearms without hesitation if they had been instructed to do so by Voigt.

The Prussian military and the imperial authorities hoped that the trial and the resulting verdict would cast a bad light on Voigt and deter possible imitators of the deed. But far from it: the court sentenced the shoemaker to "merely" four years in prison in the Tegel correctional facility. Not even his civil rights, such as the right to vote, to be elected himself, or the right to hold public office, e.g., serving as a juror in court, were taken away from him - which is very unusual in view of his criminal record.

As a mitigating factor, the court allows the fact that Voigt "after serving his last sentence had made serious and successful efforts to earn his living honestly and was well on the way to becoming a useful member of civil society."

Voigt rose to media stardom after his early release from prison in 1908. Just one day later, he immortalized his bright voice in East Prussian dialect for 200 marks on an almost three-minute gramophone recording, in which he spoke, among other things, about his thoughts during his imprisonment and addressed words of thanks to his admirers:

"Ladies and gentlemen,

If I do not speak to you publicly as a person, but only through my voice, I believe myself obliged, first of all, to express my deepest gratitude for the many proofs which you have expressed to me in this or that form during the last difficult life. [...] The lively expressions of gratitude that have come to me from all sides are a beautiful gift that you have given me in my old age. I am well aware of the value of these expressions.

[...] the longing in me to walk as a free man among free men grew ever greater. I have now become free - but I wish and pray that God may protect me from becoming free once again. Now I greet you myself from here and want to hold on to the hope that it will still be granted to me [...] to express in freer and more comprehensive speech what my life has taught me and how I have become poor in my life sometimes, but also rich sometimes - even if not in possessions and goods - than it is possible in this pressed and bound form.

And now I ask you to continue to hold me in good memory. It is gratifying and uplifting to know and feel that thousands of hearts are ready to lift, bear and forgive. As far as the external circumstances of my dismissal are concerned, the final verdict has not yet been pronounced. Good things take time!

With heartfelt greetings and old joys, Wilhelm Voigt".

Again and again, he was offered horrendous sums for an exclusive story or had to pose for a photo in his captain's uniform. In 1909, the fuss about his person took on such proportions that Voigt even had autograph cards printed, which he published at the same time as his biography " How I Became Captain of Köpenick."

As his fame gradually faded, Voigt moved to Luxembourg, where he worked mainly as a waiter and shoemaker. Thanks to his popularity, however, he was able to achieve a certain prosperity. He bought a two-seater French Lacoste & Battman, making him one of the first owners of an automobile in the Grand Duchy of Luxembourg.

During the First World War, the false captain once again comes into conflict with the Prussian military. German troops take him into custody in his new home and interrogate him. In his diary, the lieutenant in charge of this operation notes, "It remains puzzling to me how this pathetic man could once shake all of Prussia."

Friedrich-Wilhelm Voigt spent the last years of his life in solitude and seclusion in a house on the Rue du Fort Neipperg. On January 3, 1922, he died at the age of 72, completely impoverished due to the war and inflation due to lung disease.

The funeral procession encountered a squad of French soldiers at his funeral in the Liebfrauen cemetery in the Luxembourg district of Limpertsberg. When the squad leader inquires about the name of the deceased, he is answered: "Le Capitaine de Coepenick" - "The Captain of Köpenick."

Assuming that a real captain is being laid to rest, the officer orders his men to assume the posture and salute to pay their last respects to the dead "Capitaine."

To this day, the charade of Friedrich-Wilhelm Voigt remains a German myth. His grave, however, has become a place of pilgrimage, most recently due to Carl Zuckermayer's tragicomedy: "Der Hauptmann von Köpenick - ein deutsches Märchen" (The Captain of Köpenick - A German Fairy Tale).

The story has served as a model for numerous books, films, songs, and plays. Most recently, millions of viewers flocked to the cinemas in the early fifties when Heinz Rühmann marched across the screen in the role of Friedrich-Wilhelm Voigt.

Today, at the town hall in Köpenick, a life-size bronze statue by artist Spartak Babajan, as well as a permanent exhibition inside the building, commemorates the former shoemaker whose rogue prank exposed and embarrassed Kaiser Wilhelm and his unchallenged Prussian authoritarian state.

CONCLUDING WORDS OF THE AUTHOR

Dear reader,

Did you like this book? Then subscribe to my author newsletter. As a special welcome and thank you, I will give you a collection of the most disturbing cases of my True Crime book series.

In addition, if you support us with an honest review, you do us a great favor. Every review counts because it ensures that this book can be found in the great digital marketplace called Internet.

You can find the newsletter at:
https://www.subscribepage.com/truecrime

Sincerely yours Adrian Langenscheid
Instagram: @truecrimedeutschland

NEWSLETTER:

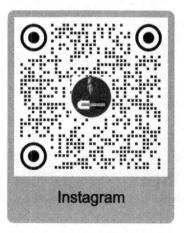

RECOMMENDATIONS

This book features the great the podcasts and authors: Mordgeflüster, True Tension, Wahre Verbrechen, Yvonne Widler, Silvana Guanziroli, Dave Grunewald, whose work I heartily recommend to all.

TRUE CRIME INTERNATIONAL:

The successful book series
by Adrian Langenscheid

His distinctive style and the success of his books made Adrian Langenscheid one of the most successful true crime authors in Germany. Did you like this book? Then feel free to order the other books in this series.

Printed in Great Britain
by Amazon

27221072R00123